THE
CHEAP CHICA'S
GUIDE TO STYLE

GOTHAM
BOOKS

THE CHEAP CHICA'S GUIDE TO STYLE

SECRETS TO SHOPPING CHEAP AND LOOKING CHIC

LILLIANA VAZQUEZ

WITH JESSICA JONES

GOTHAM BOOKS
Published by the Penguin Group
Penguin Group (USA), 375 Hudson Street,
New York, New York 10014, USA

USA | Canada | UK | Ireland | Australia |
New Zealand | India | South Africa | China
penguin.com
A Penguin Random House Company

Copyright © 2013 by Cheap Chica LLC

All illustrations copyright © 2013 by Lina Maria Carrillo

All photographs copyright © 2013 by Alison Conklin

Research by Alyssa DiSabatino

Assistant stylist: Lauren Dougherty

Cover wardrobe by H&M and Shopbop.com

LIBRARY OF CONGRESS CATALOGING-IN-PUBLICATION DATA
Vazques, Lilliana.
    The cheap chica's guide to style: secrets to shopping cheap and looking chic/ Lilliana Vazquez with Jessica Jones.
—First [edition].
        pages cm
    ISBN 978-1-592-40808-5 (pbk.)
    1. Women's clothing. 2. Fashion. 3. Shopping. I. Title.
    TT507.V375 2013
    746.9'2—dc23   2013025951

Printed in the United States of America
10 9 8 7 6 5 4 3 2 1

SET IN ADOBE GARAMOND AND DIDOT
DESIGNED BY JUDITH STAGNITTO ABBATE / ABBATE DESIGN

To my Welita, who taught me
that women should never wear pants,
and to my mom, who never took them off.

CONTENTS

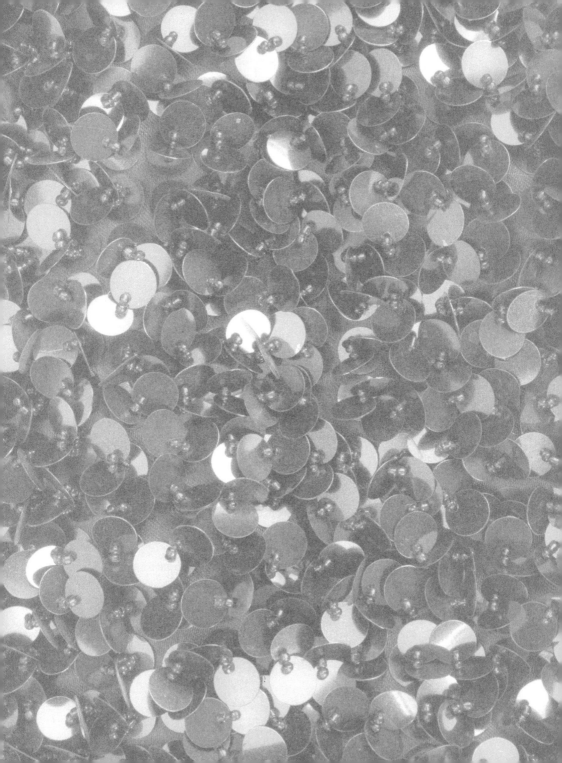

INTRODUCTION

*Finding
My Cents of
Style*

"I only paid $20!"

Since I started my career as a style expert, I can't tell you how many times I've said this phrase. It happens on a daily basis, and it still brings the biggest smile to my face. I love seeing people react in total disbelief. They can't understand how the shoes or dress they're lusting after is actually something they can afford.

As a culture obsessed with celebrity and the lives of the extravagantly wealthy, we're constantly bombarded by images of things we can't have, whether it's Victoria Beckham's collection of Birkin bags, Beyoncé's yacht, or Mariah Carey's two-thousand-square-foot closet. But we need to remember that those are just *things*, and *things* don't make you stylish. I won't name names, but there are plenty of celebrities who can afford a Birkin who have no style whatsoever. Most of the time, these *things* just mean you make a lot of money and you choose to spend it on fashion.

Over the course of my career, I've figured out how to hone my style without needing these expensive *things* to define it. I'm proud of my frugalness—so much so that I've branded myself as the Cheap Chica. And whether you're ready to admit it or not, you, too, have a little Cheap Chica in you. But just because you're thrifty in one area doesn't mean you're stingy about everything. That, my friends, is the farthest thing from the truth—although everyone is cheap about *something*. As frugal as I am about fashion, I actually don't mind spending money on things like vacations, dinners, and experiences that fit into my budget. Yet I have plenty of friends who regularly spend $1,000 a month on clothes, and if I suggest a nice dinner out . . . forget it! And don't even think about calling them cheap!

For some reason, it's become a badge of honor to spend a month's rent on a pair of shoes—but we're scared of being judged for our thriftiness. Remember: Style can't be bought. It comes from confidence and creativity. To put it in easy-to-understand fashion terms: It's not the brand of jeans you're wearing that matters—it's the way you put the rest of the outfit together and the way you carry yourself in those jeans that set you apart in a sea of denim, designer or not.

> REMEMBER: STYLE CAN'T BE BOUGHT.
> IT COMES FROM CONFIDENCE
> AND CREATIVITY.

Sadly, we live in a world where *cheap* is a bad word. People turn their noses up at shopping in stores like T.J.Maxx or Payless simply because their average price point is $19.99. No, stores like these aren't glamorous; there's no champagne while you shop, they won't give you a fancy shopping bag to carry home all of your purchases, and the clothes on the racks might even be in a state of disarray . . . but that's all fine by me, and in this book you'll learn why.

Over the years, I've learned to embrace the word *cheap* because it's saved me from wasting my hard-earned cash. As a fashion expert, I work in an industry that's built on overspending and overconsumption, but thanks to my thriftiness, I've never become a victim of it. That's because I believe anyone can look like a million bucks without breaking the bank—if you know where and how to shop and what to buy. It's taken years of practice and a lot of creativity to develop my frugal fashion formula, but I'm finally ready to share it.

• ● •

Some people are born with money. Some are born with style. A very lucky few are born with both. And then there are those who inherit neither. I fall into the last category. To help you understand where I'm coming from instead of diving right in and preaching about what you should and shouldn't wear and how you should spend your money, I'm going to share with you a condensed version of my last thirty years in the hope that it will reveal a little about who I am and in turn help you to trust me enough to put your fashion life in my hands. I'd love the opportunity to show you how to find your style without compromising who you are, or worse, the entire contents of your savings account.

I was born in 1980 in Fort Worth, Texas—not exactly the fashion capital of the world, but I'm living proof that where you're from doesn't determine where you're going! To say that my family was of moderate means is a huge understatement. Both of my parents worked tirelessly to provide for our family, so during my early years, my aunt Blanca took care of me while my mother and father were at work.

My aunt is an incredibly talented seamstress who, to this day, still finds time to make her own clothes. She was the one who taught me how to needlepoint and how to sew a garment from a pattern. We would ride the bus to our local fabric store and spend hours looking through patterns together. I thought the women on the packets looked so stylish and chic, but at that time I didn't know anyone that actually looked like them. I always left the store wondering if there were women out there who really dressed like that. The models were tall, beautiful, and glamorous—when I grew up I wanted to dress like them (particularly the ones on the Vogue patterns), and even more, I wanted to be like them. I would daydream about the life they had, what they did, and of course, what their closets looked like. Little did I know, I'd soon have to learn how to navigate their world.

My parents wanted the best education for my brother and me, and where I lived, that meant private school. My mom found a school that

likely cost as much as her yearly salary, and though my parents couldn't afford the tuition, that didn't stop them. My mom is incredibly tenacious, and she was willing to make whatever sacrifices were necessary to get me there. I enrolled at Fort Worth Country Day School in 1988 with generous help from the school's financial aid program, and before the school year even started, I realized I was in for a total culture shock.

We were required to wear uniforms at Country Day, and the school administrators sent us to their preferred vendor in an upscale neighborhood that my family wasn't too familiar with. When we got to the store, the parking lot was full of shiny

BMWs and Mercedes. My mom and I were instantly intimidated. Looking back on it, I'm sure she was thinking, *Who cares where we buy her poly-blend school uniform? How much could it really cost?* What she didn't know was that the uniform cost was just the beginning. The sales associate quickly informed us that all the girls at school monogrammed their uniforms, and being the new girl and all, I wouldn't want to feel left out. Well, duh, who wants to be the un-monogrammed new girl? She then told us that while they offered regular white and blue oxford shirts to go with the uniform, most girls opted instead for a classic Polo Ralph Lauren oxford. Of course they did!

Next we got to the shoes. School dress code dictated that they had to be leather, so my mom and I picked out classic black-and-white saddle shoes that looked perfect. I had never owned a pair like that, and even at a young age, shoes got me really excited. Cue the bubble-bursting salesperson, who explained that part of the back-to-school shopping ritual for most students was getting a new pair of Cole Haans for the year. She escorted us to a fancy armoire where they housed the shoes and showed us the latest collection. At the time, neither my mom nor I even knew shoes *came* in collections! But the second I got to the armoire, my heart started to race. The shoes were beautiful—some had tassels, some had intricately woven leather, and others were classically chic loafers. I can still remember the way the leather smelled, and I immediately started dreaming of how cute I would look in my preppy uniform and my gorgeous new designer shoes. Then, for the first time—but certainly not the last—I heard my mom utter these four words: "We can't afford it."

Up until that day, I had never really wanted for anything. We had a comfortable house. I had plenty of toys, clothes, friends, family, and everything else a little girl could want. In our social circle (which, as with most Latino families, includes only relatives) my family was considered well-off, but I suddenly came to the shocking realization that to the rest of the world, we weren't.

I didn't get the Polo shirts or the Cole Haan shoes that day, but my mom did splurge on the monogram, saying it would show off my personality and style. She promised we would take a trip to a local outlet to search for the designer items on sale. My mom wanted me to have all those nice things, but she's no sucker; there was no way she was going to pay full price.

Like mother, like daughter.

That day was just the first of many times when I would be reminded that my family couldn't afford what the kids I went to school with could. They shopped at Neiman Marcus, and we shopped at Sears. They bought new dresses for bar mitzvahs, and I had my aunt make mine. They spent thousands of dollars for new cheerleading uniforms without blinking, and my mom had to save for months to cover the cost of my new uniform each year.

During my time at Country Day, there were plenty of days when I felt different, but I quickly discovered that relationships and friendships, like style, have nothing to do with money. While my friends' *parents* could afford everything we drooled over in *Elle*, as teenagers with a weekly allowance, we certainly couldn't. My friends enlisted my help to show them how to get the look for less at our local mall, and by middle school I was already becoming quite the frugal fashionista!

In the end, sending me to private school was the best decision my family ever made. It opened my eyes to a new world and made me hungry for bigger and better experiences. It gave me the confidence and courage to take on new adventures, and along the way, I learned valuable lessons about money and budgeting—all of which helped shape who I am today.

• ● •

Fast-forward to 2002. I had just graduated from college and had moved to New York City to start my dream job at a very high-end fashion magazine. The magazine, which is still published today, is targeted at the very wealthy, who have extra money to spend on really expensive (often unnecessary) things, like $2,000 Missoni bikinis and $100,000 sharkskin handbags that were deemed the season's must-have items.

You're probably asking yourself: *Why would she want to work at a place like that?*

Good question. It was like being at my private school all over again, except with even richer kids in even better clothes. But at the time, it was also the pinnacle of the fashion world. For someone who loves fashion as much as I do, there wasn't a better place to be. I was inspired every day by the creativity and passion of the entire editorial team.

Unfortunately, I wasn't a part of that team. Instead, I worked on the business side of the magazine as a lowly ad-sales assistant (which mostly entailed a lot of errand running for my boss). Every day I was reminded of how lucky I was to have my job and of the thousands of girls who would give anything to be me—as if fetching salmon salads (the "rich in omega-3s" diet was big at the time) for my boss and researching the best organic,

Dollars & Sense

Does the thought of boots with a corset detail make you cringe? That's because they were trendy—in 2002! Think about that the next time you want to drop $200 on a pair of neon platforms. Will you be regretting your investment next year—or even next season?

hypoallergenic, side-sleeping pillow for her to use was a great use of my business degree.

I lasted only six months there for a multitude of reasons, and while it wasn't the greatest experience, I wouldn't trade my time there for the world. That job took my love for fashion to a whole new level; it introduced me to new designers and a new way of dressing, and it really helped shape my personal style. Most important, though, it was home to my greatest "look for less" moment.

A snotty woman in my department had a penchant for wearing high-end designer shoes and making faces at assistants like me. She had a great career and, in turn, a closet full of overpriced designer clothes and shoes. She showed up to work one day in a pair of knee-high black leather boots that had a corset detail up the back. (Remember, this was 2002.) They were a little on the trendy side but still gorgeous, and they happened to look exactly like the pair I was wearing that day.

One of the ad directors saw me walking by and said, "OMG. You and Jenny"—names have been changed to protect the not so innocent—"have

[

LABELS DON'T DEFINE US—THEY'RE JUST LITTLE PIECES OF CLOTH THAT TELL YOU HOW TO TAKE CARE OF YOUR GARMENT.

]

on the same boots today! Jenny, get over here!" Before I could tell her that I was sure Jenny and I were *not* wearing the same boots, Jenny walked in.

With a snarl, she said, "Wow, that must have been a really big purchase for someone like you."

Someone like me? What was I—some mutant from the planet Poor? Determined not to give her the satisfaction of seeing me upset, I composed myself and replied, "Actually they weren't at all. I got these for $49.99 at Century 21. Are yours BCBGeneration too?"

They weren't. They were Jimmy Choos (natch), and the woman almost died on the spot. This little label game proved a lesson my mother taught me, one that I have long subscribed to: A designer name is just a name; if you can afford it, more power to you, and if you can't, don't sweat it.

While I'm not the biggest sports fan, I can't help but use a little sports analogy here. Throughout this book, think of yourself as the quarterback on the field of fashion and me as your head coach. I can't guarantee you'll score a touchdown every time you shop or get dressed, but I'll give you the necessary tools and training to have a winning strategy. These next seven chapters are my personal playbook, and in my game, anyone can afford to look good. Remember: Labels don't define us—they're just little pieces of cloth that tell you how to take care of your garment.

Think Chic

Someone like you: Though my coworker's words were shocking, we know what she meant: An entry-level employee shouldn't be expected to afford the same luxuries as a top-tier manager. (Though that doesn't mean you can't look like you do!) Be realistic about your financial situation and adjust your price points accordingly. When we talk about splurges later on, that might mean a $100 purchase to you, while it could mean a $1,000 purchase to someone else.

THE STARTING LINE

Chapter 1

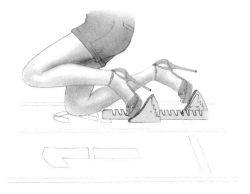

There are certain words we've come to recognize as bad words. You know the ones. The words you'd never say around your mother or your pastor. The ones you use symbols like #&@ and * to spell out in work e-mails so you don't get flagged by your IT department. The ones you say when you stub your toe against your bed frame. *Those* words. Somewhere along the way, *che@p* became one of *those* words, and I'm single-handedly trying to redefine it!

While some people prefer to hide their cheapness, I like to let my cheap flag fly, and I want to help you be proud of your savvy style too. But in order to help you unlock the secrets of shopping cheap and looking chic, first we need to identify what type of shopper you are. Take the following quiz to get a better sense of your spending style.

[WHILE SOME PEOPLE PREFER TO HIDE THEIR CHEAPNESS, I LIKE TO LET MY CHEAP FLAG FLY.]

WHAT KIND OF CHICA ARE YOU?

1. You're at the mall and you see the perfect leather jacket, priced way out of your budget. You . . .

a. walk right past it, headed straight for the movie theater.

b. buy it with zero hesitation. Every celebrity is wearing these Acne jackets right now!

c. ogle it, pet the leather, and vow to start saving your money so you can come back and get it in a few months.

d. get it . . . then return it two days later. Luckily, on your way out of the store, you see another one just like it for much less—and you deserve a pick-me-up after the week you've had!

2. When your credit card bill comes every month, you . . .

a. pay it off in full. No carried balances here!

b. pay the minimum balance. You'll have money one day, but right now, this is the only way to maintain the kind of lifestyle you want.

c. pay as much as you can for the next few months until you cover the cost of the Céline purse you splurged on.

d. *were* ready to pay it off in full, but then you went on that shopping spree when you and your boyfriend broke up . . .

3. Do brand names and designers matter to you?

a. Nope! As long as it looks OK, I don't care
where it came from.

b. Definitely. I wouldn't be caught dead in a
no-name label.

c. Sometimes, but I have a mixture of high-
end and low-end items in my closet.

d. I don't care too much about where it came
from; I just love that high I get from buying
something new.

4. When do you do most of your shopping?

a. Only when there's something I absolutely
need.

b. The question is, when *don't* I shop?

c. When I get a notice telling me my favorite store is having a sale.

d. When I get a promotion at work—I earned it!

5. How do you rationalize your spending?

a. No need to justify anything—I got only the item I needed at a price that was
within my budget.

b. When I'm older, I won't care as much about how I look. Now is the time to
dress my best!

c. I brought my lunch to work every day this week so that I could get the bracelet
I'd been eyeing.

d. My friends all dress a certain way, and it's not fair that I shouldn't be able to,
too.

6. Your go-to button-down shirt is starting to look a little worse for the wear. What do you do?

a. Keep wearing it regardless. I want to get as much mileage out of it as I can before having to shell out for a replacement.
b. Head straight to Theory to pick up another.
c. Disguise it as best I can under blazers and with bold accessories until the Gap e-mails me a coupon.
d. Go buy one . . . along with a new skirt, belt, and watch to wear with it! I lost three pounds this week, so I'm feeling good!

[RESULTS]

If you answered mostly A's,
YOU'RE A SALE-ONLY CHICA.

This Chica is frugal and always diligent about her purchases. She most likely pays her credit card off every month and doesn't spend money she doesn't have. Fashion may or may not play a large role in her day-to-day life. She likely doesn't realize that having style doesn't have to mean breaking the bank, or she doesn't see the value in dressing her best.

If this sounds like you, flip straight to page 18 for a style self-evaluation and a preview of how this book can help you expand your fervor for fashion (while still being financially responsible). Be sure to check out the description of your style sister, Sensible Chica, on page 27, as well—you might find that you can learn a thing or two from her, too!

If you answered mostly B's,
YOU'RE A SPLURGE CHICA.

This Chica loves fashion and worships labels. She has to have something if it's the latest trend or the hottest brand. She generally doesn't think about the cost and is willing to have credit card debt to get what she needs and keep up with her crew fashionwise. She needs to learn what havoc her spending habits might have on her financial future and be educated in all the lower-cost options that exist.

Is this you? If so, turn to page 22, where I'll give you some straight talk and tell you just what you're going to gain (and save) by reading the next six chapters. It might also be beneficial for you to learn from the mistakes of your wobbly-willpowered partner in crime, Spontaneous Chica, whom I'll address on page 30.

If you answered mostly C's,
YOU'RE A SENSIBLE CHICA.

This is a Chica who loves to shop, enjoys fashion, and likes having nice things—but she does it within her financial limits. She saved long and hard for her Miu Miu leather jacket, and she'd be devastated to know that the same coat sold for nearly half the price online. Though she's a good mix of sense and style, she could make her money go further by educating herself on other options.

If that describes you and your spending habits, turn to page 27, where I'll give you a (much-deserved) pat on the back for your balanced approach to fashion but also detail the secrets we'll uncover in this book that will help your style and your budget stretch even further. There's also some worthwhile advice for you in the breakdown on page 18 of the Sale-Only Chica, whose shopping strategy is not unlike your own.

If you answered mostly D's,
YOU'RE A SPONTANEOUS CHICA.

Whether she's bored or just in need of retail therapy, this Chica shops with her emotions, spending money she doesn't necessarily have on things she doesn't necessarily need. It's important that she recognize her spending habits and learn new and helpful ways to shop more for what she really needs and less to fill a void.

If this sounds familiar, go to page 30, where I'll give you some advice on how to put a stop to these dangerous habits now and outline the valuable information you're going to receive in this book. You can also gain some insight from the description of the Splurge Chica—who suffers from a lot of the same tendencies that you do—on page 22.

[ ]

THE
BREAKDOWN

If You're a Sale-Only Chica

Are you sure you're a flesh-and-blood human? Your ability to resist the temptation to overspend is admirable—and your perfect credit score and robust savings account speak for themselves. You're so careful with your spending that it's hard to find room to criticize, except to remind you that you deserve something special every now and then. The same way dieticians advise you to have a cookie if you're craving one rather than deprive yourself and risk overindulging later, it's OK to treat yourself to something nice, as long as you do so in moderation.

But is it really just your admirable restraint that keeps you from overspending? Is the real problem that you're so busy that you don't have time to think about how you look? Are you stressed by the time and effort shopping can take? Don't worry—in Chapter 4, I'll help you minimize your shopping time by identifying what to look for and when to shop for it. I'll also introduce you to websites and apps in Chapter 6 that take the guesswork out of buying, and you'll get practical guides in Chapter 7 that will make putting an outfit together quick and easy.

Or it could be that fashion simply isn't a big part of your daily life. Maybe you think it's silly to worry about what you wear. True, while clothes certainly don't make a person, they *can* make a big difference in the way the world sees you. At work, the way you present yourself can have huge ramifications. If you show up looking sloppy, you could be sending a message that you lack ambition. Your mismatched earrings could signal an inattention to detail. The way you dress can also have a huge effect on

[IF YOU SHOW UP LOOKING SLOPPY, YOU COULD BE SENDING A MESSAGE THAT YOU LACK AMBITION.]

your confidence. You can't deny that when you look good, you feel good! And when you're wearing clothes that make you feel your best, you might be more likely to say hi to a friendly looking guy on the subway or to speak up in a meeting. Now, that's a win-win!

Bottom line: There's absolutely nothing shameful in caring about how you look. It isn't shallow; it's taking pride in yourself and your appearance. So in Chapter 2, I'm going to help you identify exactly what your style is so you know whom to emulate and what items to look for when you shop. Together, we'll shed those negative stigmas so you're not afraid to show off just how fantastic you are.

Lastly, if you're unhappy with your body, I know that shopping probably isn't the number one thing on your to-do list. Those 360-degree mirrors and harsh lighting would illuminate flaws even on Gisele

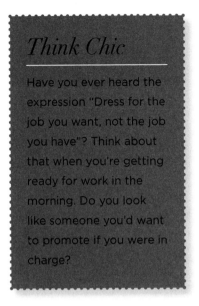

Bündchen (or at least I like to imagine that they would). But squeezing into clothes that have gotten two sizes too small simply because you dread going to look for new ones won't do anything but accentuate the extra pounds you've added to your midsection. While the process might be painful at times, finding clothes that fit and flatter your body will help you be OK with the way you look. In the long run, you'll be happy you did it. To help, in Chapter 2, I'll identify key clothing items that will flatter *your* figure based on your body type. I'll also give you shopping strategies in Chapter 4 that will make a trip to the mall, a boutique, or a secondhand store easy and productive. In Chapter 6, I'll give you the ultimate buyer's guide to online retailers so you don't even have to leave your house to shop if you don't want to! And since I know being responsible with your money is important to you (as it is for all good Cheap Chicas), in Chapter 5, I'll tell you which items you should spend a little more than you're used to on, and which are acceptable to save on.

Whatever is causing your lagging interest in fashion, Sale-Only Chica, here are some pointers to help make a shopping trip stress-free and successful:

- **LOOK HOT.** I've never understood people who go to the mall in work-out clothes. You're not going to like the way anything looks when your hair is in a sweaty ponytail and you've got socks and sneakers peeking out from beneath your cocktail dress! Put on some makeup, fix your hair, and wear an outfit that makes you feel stylish and sexy. That feeling will carry over when you're trying on new clothes.

- **STRIP SMARTER.** Don't wear knee-high boots over jeans and lots of jewelry when you shop—you're just going to have to take it all off when you try on clothes and put it back on again when you're through. Wear items that are easy to get on and off, so you don't skip a trip to the dressing room just to avoid the hassle of getting undressed.

- **THINK AHEAD.** If you're trying on work slacks that you'd typically wear with pumps, wear shoes of similar height (or bring a pair with you if you can't bear the thought of cruising the mall in four-inch heels). Have a strapless bra on if you're looking for gowns. And if you're trying on bikinis, leave the granny panties at home!

- **ASK FOR HELP.** Shopping can be overwhelming. If you're looking for a particular piece and you're not spotting it easily, don't get discouraged and walk out. A sales rep will be able to point you in the right direction— and perhaps suggest something you wouldn't normally have considered.

- **USE A STYLIST.** Some stores, like J.Crew and Nordstrom, offer complimentary stylist services, so take them up on it. (I'll cover these services more in depth in Chapter 6.) And don't be intimidated! A stylist's job is to make you look your best, so he or she will help you find clothes that will flatter your frame and can offer advice on what works best for you. Then you can take that knowledge to other stores.

If You're a Splurge Chica

Y ou, friend, need a fashion intervention! You've got a great eye for style, no doubt, but your shopping habits and your disregard for your finances are going to get you in trouble someday. It's not totally your fault—we know how hard it is to see supermodels strutting the runways in

[THERE'S MORE TO LIFE
THAN LOUIS VUITTON.]

this season's hottest styles and not covet those items. But there's more to life than Louis Vuitton. I swear.

How many times have you used the phrase "I have to have it"? I know I'm guilty! But by convincing ourselves that we *need* something when we really just *want* it—no matter how badly—we're trying to justify the purchase to ourselves. Sure, we need clothes to protect ourselves from the elements (not to mention the laws that prevent you from going out in your birthday suit). But you know as well as I do that there are much more affordable ways to cover up than with a TSE cashmere sweater.

The biggest challenge for you is to reverse your thinking. Instead of being proud of your expensive purchases, be proud of the bargains you find! Remember: Spending a lot of money is easy. Any dummy with a trust fund can do it. But you shouldn't have to spend a million bucks to look like a million bucks. It takes a lot more skill and imagination to look that way for $100. I'll help you in Chapter 5 by identifying which items are worth a higher price tag and which you really need to cut back on. And in Chapter 7, I'll give you practical ideas for how to mix your high-end purchases with low-end steals for a look that still reads expensive—and a few simple tricks to make it look like you were styled by a pro.

You know how movies that are inspired by a true story are often just as good—or better—than the real thing? Take a Hollywood approach to your fashion: Rather than having to have the exact designer item, let yourself be *inspired* by the looks you see in high-end stores or fashion magazines. So instead of spending a fortune on a pair of flats, your shoes can be based on a true Tory (Burch, that is).

When you do splurge on a big-ticket item, make

> ## *Fashion Fact*
>
> Feel like you could spend days at the mall? You do! On average, American women shop for 399 hours and 49 minutes each year. That adds up to more than sixteen days!

> ## *Haute Hint*
>
> To help keep your spending in check, purchase a Visa or American Express prepaid card and load it with as much as your budget allots for clothing. When the money runs out, you're done shopping for the month!

sure you'll be able to get a lot of wear out of it. More and more, the fashion world is embracing recycling, and I'm not just talking about newspapers and aluminum cans (although that type of recycling is important too). Celebrities like Michelle Obama and Catherine, Duchess of Cambridge (aka **Kate Middleton**)—highly photographed women who aren't afraid to repeat what they wear—are constant examples of how a different shoe, jacket, or accessory can give an outfit an entirely new look. If they can be seen in the same dress twice, so can you. In the photo section in the middle of the book, I'm going to show you how to turn thirteen items into a month's worth of looks for each season. I'll also take five items that you may already have in your closet and show you three very different ways to wear them, depending on how adventurous (in the fashion sense) you're feeling.

If you're still having trouble with the idea of giving up your designer brands, the simplest bit of advice I could give you is to look for the brands you love at bargain prices. You might be shocked to know that websites like RueLaLa.com, consignment shops, and off-price stores such as T.J.Maxx and Marshalls have well-known names at considerably lower-than-retail prices. Chapter 6 is going to be your go-to reference guide for all manner of discount stores and sites.

But I want to push you even further, Splurge Chica. I'm going to teach you to branch out of your cushy comfort zone and make your money work for you! We're going to start later in this chapter by helping you set—and keep—a realistic budget. Then in Chapter 3, I'm going to help you take inventory of your wardrobe and learn how to display it in a functional, appealing way so that you don't spend money unnecessarily. And in Chapter 4, I'm going to help you generate a shopping list to keep yourself in line when you need reining in and give you a number of shopping strategies so you can outsmart retailers and their crafty tactics. A few other things you should keep in mind:

- **TLC GOES A LONG WAY.** Rather than blowing cash on replacement items when your clothes get worn down, help the clothes you already have go the distance by taking care of them properly or having them updated by a tailor according to changing styles. Even a hole in a sweater isn't a deal breaker—a reweaver can work miracles on a tear, borrowing threads from elsewhere on the garment to reconstruct the damaged area. Most times, you can't even tell any work has been done on the finished product.

- **SPEND VERSUS SAVE.** I'm going to teach you which items are worth spending more money on—and which aren't—in Chapter 5. Here's a hint: Remember those corset-detail boots my coworker and I both had on at my magazine gig? Who do you think was sadder when that trend went out of style? Me, who'd spent $50, or my coworker, who'd dropped $1,500 on them?

- **DO YOUR RESEARCH.** Before you show up at a store, do a little bit of research so you know which brands, styles, and looks you're interested in. If you can narrow down your options in advance, you're much less likely to get distracted and buy something unnecessary when you get to the store. I'll go into this more deeply in Chapter 4.

- **MAKE A DATE.** Try to shop just before you have plans. Sometimes simply having somewhere to be and keeping your browsing time to a minimum is the best way to go easy on your wallet.

If You're a Sensible Chica

Y ou strike the right balance between splurgy and stingy. You appreciate the finer things and aren't afraid to indulge now and then, but you know that this requires sacrificing in other areas. Of course, that doesn't mean you're always the model of perfect shopping habits, but you work to keep the cravings in check, supplementing your wardrobe with plenty of more affordable pieces.

But just because you're sensible doesn't mean you're shopping as intelligently as you could be. That's where I come in. If I told you I could help you find that handbag you scrimped and saved for at half the price somewhere else (and I will, in Chapter 6), or that if you'd just waited another month, you could've gotten it at a closeout price (more on this in Chapter 4), would you be interested? Or what if I could help you find one that looks exactly like it for dimes on the dollar? (I can: I'll tell you where to look in Chapter 6!) You can save yourself some of the effort of pinching pennies simply by knowing what's out there and when to look for it.

In this book, I'm going to show you how to elevate yourself from "sensible" to "sensational," all without spending any more than you're already spending now. In Chapter 2, I'll help you define your style and identify what pieces work best for you. In Chapters 4 and 6, I'll teach you advanced tips for shopping smarter—from what times to shop to get the

[I'M GOING TO SHOW YOU HOW TO ELEVATE YOURSELF FROM "SENSIBLE" TO "SENSATIONAL."]

best deals to how to use technology to make sure there's not a better price lurking out there somewhere. In Chapter 3, I'll help you see what wonders you have hiding in your closet, and in Chapter 7, I'll teach you how to mix and match them in inventive ways to get multiple looks from the same item—or how simple alterations can create a whole new piece! I'll cull advice from the experts and share knowledge I've learned over my years in the industry to turn you, Sensible Chica, into a style expert of your own!

Consider the following:

- **BREAK A HABIT.** Do you find yourself going into the same five stores when you go to the mall? On one hand, knowing which places are more likely to carry items you'll like will cut down on shopping time. But by sticking to what you know, you could be missing out on tons of great hidden finds! If you like J.Crew, for instance, have you been into LOFT lately? They're both incorporating the same elements and color palettes into their designs, but LOFT is considerably cheaper.

- **GO ROGUE.** Who says we ladies have to stick to the ladies' section? Juniors' sections often carry trendy items at prices lower than their more mature counterparts, while boys' departments are great for oversized shirts and sweaters, comfy tees and blazers.

> DON'T BE AFRAID TO BOLDLY GO
> WHERE YOU THINK NO THIRTY-YEAR-OLD
> HAS GONE BEFORE!

- **DON'T JUDGE A BOOK BY ITS COVER.** Do you walk right past Charlotte Russe or Forever 21 because you think you'll be the oldest person in the store? So what? Don't be afraid to boldly go where you think no thirty-year-old has gone before! (And believe me, *plenty* have.) You won't feel embarrassed when you get tons of compliments on your fab new dress, especially when you know you got it for $16.80 on the clearance rack.

- **UPGRADE.** So you found an adorable skirt that has the same shape and swing as the Tibi one you'd been drooling over, but it's missing a few crucial details. Who says you can't add your own bells and whistles? A tailor may be able to add an exposed zipper or a slit where you want it, while, with a simple needle and thread, you can easily change the buttons to make something look more expensive.

If You're a Spontaneous Chica

While some people are emotional eaters, you're an emotional shopper. For you, the process of going shopping is less about finding what you need and more about self-medicating. Some people shop when they're upset: Whether you're sad over a fight with a friend, frustrated with your mother-in-law, or angry that you didn't get a promotion, the only way you can think to make it better is to buy yourself something new. Others shop when they're happy, to reward themselves for a job well done at the office or to look extra special for a night out on the town. Still others shop simply out of boredom: When there's nothing to do, heading to the mall seems like a better option than sitting at home twiddling their thumbs. It could also be insecurity and a sense of competitiveness that make you feel the need to try to keep up with the Joneses (or the Kardashians, as the case may be). If your coworker shows up wearing the most fabulous Brian Atwood pumps, you've got to have a pair too.

Whatever the motivation, emotional shopping is an unhealthy practice that not only won't help your pocketbook but also won't address the underlying issues that are leading you to seek retail therapy.

First, it's important to identify which type of emotional shopper you are. When do you find yourself being tempted to spend? What's going on in your life at that moment that prompts the need to buy something? Talk to a friend or family member about what you're going through. Ask him or her to be there for you and to hold you accountable. If the problem is more serious—if you're suffering from depression or have been impacted by a real trauma—please put this book down and contact a professional. Fashion is fun; it's not a cure.

The most important thing to remember is this: Though going on a shopping spree can make you feel good for the moment, when you get home and start unpacking all your purchases (and mentally tallying all your expenditures), you may start to feel a renewed sense of guilt. And how have you, Spontaneous Chica, learned to make yourself feel better? More shopping! Without realizing it, you've set a vicious cycle in motion.

Luckily, you can curb these bad habits simply by educating yourself on better, more responsible ways to shop and spend. The first step is to set a budget, which I'll show you how to do later in this chapter. As we'll discuss in Chapter 2, it's also important to buy clothes that make sense for your body type and your lifestyle rather than wildly unrealistic clothing

> ## Fashion Fact
>
> What if I told you that every time you went shopping, you were gaining weight (in your closet)? The average woman buys half her weight in apparel annually.

that makes you feel better just for the moment. In Chapter 3, you'll rediscover your closet, because knowing exactly what you have eliminates any excuse to buy repeats simply for the sake of buying something. You'll learn the tricks of savvy shoppers in Chapter 4, and in Chapter 6 you'll discover retailers—both brick-and-mortar and online—with prices so low that your money will go further. And when you learn in Chapter 7 how to make multiple outfits out of the pieces you already own, you might feel less tempted to buy something new when you're feeling down—instead, you can focus your energy on creatively remixing your wardrobe.

You can also try these tips:

- **HIT RETURN.** If you're prone to emotional spending, make sure you're buying only from stores that have a reasonable return policy—and that doesn't mean exchanges or store credit only. This way, when you emerge from your funk and change your mind about your purchases, you can put that money back where it belongs: in your wallet! Though buying in bulk and returning later isn't a habit you want to get into—inevitably, a few of those items find their way into your closet—sometimes the high of getting your money back feels almost as good as buying in the first place.

- **SAVE YOUR RECEIPTS.** As soon as I get home from a shopping trip or a package arrives from an online buying spree, I immediately file the receipts in an envelope marked with the month so that, if I do change my mind, I know exactly where they are. It makes returns easier and a lot less stressful.

- **RECONNECT.** As much as you may love your clothes, they're not going to be there for you when you need a shoulder to lean on.

Strengthen your social circle and spend time with friends, or call loved ones who live far away. Laughing over drinks or reminiscing about old times with a pal will give you the great feeling you've been searching for.

- **HOLLY HOBBY.** Where do your passions lie? (Outside of shopping, I mean!) Whatever your interests, find something that you love to do and make a hobby out of it. Paint, write poetry, or rearrange your furniture. Learn to play the guitar or take a photography class. Volunteer for a charity or organize a running club. It doesn't matter what it is—just find something healthier to invest your time and money in. Thirty years from now, you'll be happy you learned how to make a mean marinara sauce, while you most definitely won't be wearing the Herve Leger bandage dress you bought on a whim in Vegas.

- **RETHINK REWARDS.** When something great happens at work or you accomplish a personal goal, you deserve a little something to reward yourself—the key word here being *little*! If you quit smoking, treat yourself to a nice meal or a fantastic bottle of wine. When you work overtime all month to meet a deadline, a well-earned massage is the perfect way to unwind. But nothing is worth a shopping spree that undoes all of your hard work and saving.

[
THIRTY YEARS FROM NOW, YOU WON'T BE WEARING THE HERVE LEGER BANDAGE DRESS YOU BOUGHT ON A WHIM IN VEGAS.
]

- **HAVE FUN WITH FUNDS.** Monitor your money closely and watch it start to accumulate when you cut out the spontaneous spending. Seeing the numbers start to grow will encourage you to keep up the good work.

• • •

Now that you know what kind of shopper you are, perhaps the best place to start when deciding what you can spend is the dreaded B-word. That's right: I'm talking about setting a budget. Now, I know it can be daunting (not to mention a little bit of a buzzkill) to really be honest about your spending and to set limits for yourself, but it truly is the best way to know how much flexible income you have to work with and to keep yourself from living beyond your means. Besides, the peace of mind you'll have knowing that you're not throwing away your hard-earned cash is, like they say in the MasterCard commercials, priceless.

You might be asking yourself, *Why is budgeting so important? Thanks to the magic of credit cards, I can afford to play today and pay tomorrow!*

Stop right there, Chica. Let me go ahead and bust that myth before we get any further into this section. Sure, credit cards can be a great tool for saving money, especially since almost every store nowadays offers one with its own reward program. But used irresponsibly, credit cards can actually do the opposite, costing you more in the long run.

Fashion Fact

Ever wonder who came up with the dreaded word *budget*? It comes from the French *bougette* or *bouge*, which translates to *leather bag.*

Break Bad Spending Habits Forever

No one's perfect when it comes to spending money. We're all subject to the seductive powers of a top that drapes just right or a skirt that hugs our curves. The important thing is to know your weaknesses and enable yourself to overcome them. Break common bad spending habits with these pointers:

1. Go cash only.

Credit cards make it easy to overspend, but you can't use them if you don't have them with you. Leave the plastic at home and stick to cash for all your purchases.

2. Shop with a list.

Ever gone into a store for a few items and emerged with a bundle of bags? We all have. Fortunately there's an easy fix for this common spending trap: Shop with a list—and stick to it! We'll talk more about how to make a list in Chapter 4.

3. Allowances aren't just for kids.

Look over your budget and decide how much money you can afford to blow each week. Then withdraw this amount from your checking account at the beginning of the week, and you can spend guilt-free all week long! When the money's gone, the spending stops—no exceptions.

4. Play the waiting game.

Before making any purchase over your personal threshold, give yourself at least forty-eight hours to think it over. This will give you time to decide whether you really need—and can actually afford—the object of your affection. Can't stop thinking about it two days later? Go get it—but save your receipt. You never know when you might change your mind.

5. Find a shopping buddy (who spends less than you).

If you have a hard time saying no (like me), enlist the help of a friend every time you shop—just make sure your friend isn't an enabler and will help you save more often than you spend! If you're an addict, think of your friend as your smart shopping sponsor!

6. Remember that a little goes a long way.

Three-dollar lattes may not put you in debt, but you'll be surprised how quickly those little expenditures add up! To help wean yourself off the habit, start saving for something you really want—a Chanel bag, a tropical vacation, or paying off that student loan in half the time. Remind yourself of this goal each time you feel tempted to blow money on your habit, and before you know it, you'll have reached your goal!

Let's say you went digging through the racks at T.J.Maxx and found a Michael Kors bag that was marked down from $300 to $100. What a steal, right? Well, if you purchase the bag with cash or you use a credit card and pay your balance in full at the end of the month, you are, in fact, getting a great deal. But if you pay just part of the bill, the minimum amount, or nothing at all, you could end up paying a lot more than $100 in the end. Think about this:

The average major credit card has an annual percentage rate of 17 percent. Store credit cards often carry rates that are even higher, with the average somewhere around 24 percent. Every month that goes by before you pay that bill in full, the more you pay in interest on that $100 bag. The more you put on that card, the more interest you end up paying in the long run. And if you ignore your bills completely, paying nothing at

Dollars & Sense

Don't let credit cards fool you into paying more than the sticker price. Compare the cost of these items to what you'll pay after a year of interest*:

ITEM	PRICE	WITH 1 YEAR'S INTEREST
Essie nail polish	$8	$9.35
MAC false eyelashes	$16	$18.70
Seven jeans	$175	$204.56
Nicole Miller coat	$300	$350.67
Max Mara cashmere sweater	$700	$818.23
Herve Leger bandage dress	$1,400	$1,636.46

*Using an average interest rate of 16.89 percent

all because you can't afford to make a payment, you can get into even more serious trouble.

I know this all too well. In 2002, I took a spring break trip that I knew I couldn't afford. But I wasn't going to miss a vacation in the Dominican Republic with my best girlfriends! Instead, I just put it on plastic, charging $1,200 for the five-day trip. When I couldn't pay the bill at the end of the month (and for many subsequent months), the lender declared my account a write-off, ruining my credit for the next six years. No matter how much fun I had dancing *bachata* and sipping Miami Vices on the Punta Cana beach, it wasn't worth the financial damage and personal humiliation it cost me.

How It Works: Credit Card Write-offs

When someone fails to make payments on their credit card for at least six months, a credit card company can declare the account a write-off, which reduces the company's tax liability and puts a major dent in your credit score—but doesn't excuse you from paying the balance.

Cracking the Credit Score Code

Think your credit card spending is your little secret? Think again. Your credit score—which is determined by how responsibly you use your credit cards, among other factors—can affect a lot of things down the road.

To help you understand just what a credit score is and how it can impact you, I asked Anthony M. David, a Washington, D.C.–based financial adviser and vice president of a major wealth management firm, to provide a crash course on credit.

Q: What is a credit score?

A: Your credit score is a number determined by a mathematical equation that signifies how reliable you will be as a borrower of money. It's based on payment history, outstanding debt, length of credit history, pursuit of new credit, and types of credit used.

Q: How important is having a good credit score?

A: It's extremely important, as credit scores are used for obtaining credit cards, auto loans, and mortgages. Many people are surprised to find out that insurance companies, utility companies, and even employers look at them as well.

Q: What's an average credit score, and what's considered a good score?

A: There are varying opinions as to what the "average" credit score is in the United States, but most sources indicate that with scores between 580 and 720, a loan can often be secured. A score above 720 is very good.

The point of being a Cheap Chica is to be smart about how you spend so you get to keep more in the bank. It's all the more reason to be honest about your finances and outline a budget for yourself. To do this, start by tracking your spending for several months—think of it as a food journal for your fashion—an exercise that, admittedly, can be a very sobering experience. Organize your expenditures by category. Some of these will be fixed (meaning they don't change much for the most part), such as your rent or mortgage, car payment, and phone bill. Others will be variable, meaning they can vary greatly from month to month.

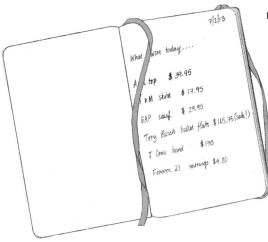

Some of these expenditures will be necessities, while others will be luxuries, and it's important to know the difference. A luxury doesn't necessarily mean a spa day at the Ritz-Carlton; it could be a $5 Mocha Ice Blended at Coffee Bean (my fave!). It simply means something we don't *need*. Necessities, on the other hand, are things like food, electricity, and gasoline for your car—items we can't live without. And believe it or not, you *can* live without weekly manicures!

Despite the shifts in your variable spending, after some time, you can figure out an average for what you typically spend in each category in a given thirty-day period. Once you've averaged your monthly expenses, add them up and compare them to your total income. If you're spending more than you're making, it's time to take a hard look at your habits and

[A LUXURY DOESN'T NECESSARILY MEAN A SPA DAY AT THE RITZ-CARLTON; IT COULD BE A $5 MOCHA ICE BLENDED AT COFFEE BEAN (MY FAVE!).]

decide which you can really afford to keep. Prioritize your spending and set realistic limits for yourself. It may make you feel good to say you're going to spend only $100 a month on clothes, but if you find yourself going over budget every month, what's the point? It's better to set achievable goals that you can actually stick to, so at the end of each month, you can be proud of what you've accomplished.

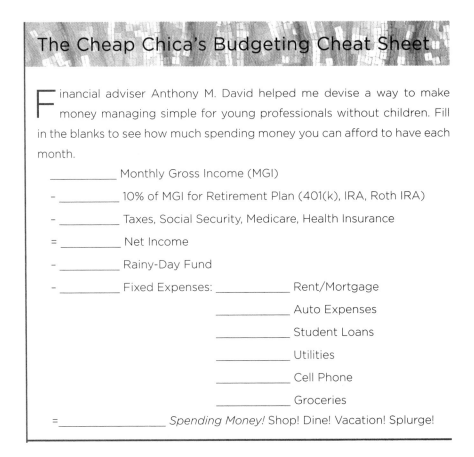

The Cheap Chica's Budgeting Cheat Sheet

Financial adviser Anthony M. David helped me devise a way to make money managing simple for young professionals without children. Fill in the blanks to see how much spending money you can afford to have each month.

_____ Monthly Gross Income (MGI)

- _____ 10% of MGI for Retirement Plan (401(k), IRA, Roth IRA)

- _____ Taxes, Social Security, Medicare, Health Insurance

= _____ Net Income

- _____ Rainy-Day Fund

- _____ Fixed Expenses: _____ Rent/Mortgage

_____ Auto Expenses

_____ Student Loans

_____ Utilities

_____ Cell Phone

_____ Groceries

=_____ *Spending Money!* Shop! Dine! Vacation! Splurge!

Don't forget to make sure that a portion of your monthly income—many experts suggest 10 percent—is going into a retirement account. That way, you can still be the best-dressed lady years from now when you've got blue hair and you're living in a retirement community! (Try the 401(k) calculator at Bloomberg.com to see just how much your money can grow.)

I'm not going to tell you that you have to deprive yourself of all luxuries; I'm simply saying you have to be reasonable about them and account for them using what's left of your paycheck once your necessary spending has been totaled. I'll confess, for instance, that I absolutely hate blow-drying my hair. It's thick and has a slight wave, which makes it a styling nightmare—I'm constantly walking the line between fabulous and frizzy. So I leave the blow-drying to the professionals, splurging on—I can't believe I'm about to admit this—a weekly $35 blowout. That's $140 a month! (I told you this process can be sobering!)

It may seem crazy to spend so much on hair. (At least that's what my husband tells me.) But like all good Cheap Chicas, I have a monthly budget for personal grooming, including haircuts and color, mani/pedis, waxing, facials, massages, and, of course, blowouts, which works out to approximately $75 a week. To make sure I meet my budget, I do most of my remaining grooming at home, rarely springing for things like massages and getting a haircut only about twice a year.

The point is, there's no such thing as a one-size-fits-all budget. Where you want to spend and where you want to save is up to you. It's just about deciding what's important to you and allocating your resources appropriately—and then having a plan to cover the expenditure!

When it comes to budgeting, the Internet can be your best friend. There are lots of useful websites and apps that offer guidance and keep you on pace.

> ## Fashion Fact
>
> Per year, the average American woman spends:
>
> - $217 on makeup
> - $417 on body-care products
> - $1,069 on clothing
> - $250 on shoes

Dollars & Sense

Pull out that piggy bank from your childhood—spare change can really add up! Some banks have programs that automatically transfer the change from each transaction into your savings account. You'll be surprised how fast those pennies can multiply.

One of the sites I use is Mint.com, which I discovered in 2007 when I was planning my wedding. Not only did the site likely save my marriage, but it also rescued me from budget purgatory! The thing I love about it, in addition to the fact that it's completely free to use, is that it works for those of us who aren't numbers people. It automatically categorizes your spending and presents the information in easy-to-understand pie charts. From there, you can track where your money is going and set limits for different categories. It even sends you e-mails when you've gone over your limits—an immensely helpful (if sometimes annoying) tool in understanding and accepting your boundaries.

Once you've got an efficient and realistic budget working for you, the key is sticking to it. When you start to see your bank balance grow, it can be more tempting to spend, but don't let that money start to burn a hole in your checking account! One way I've made this easier for me is by moving all my accumulated cash into a savings account. I purposely don't link a debit card to it, which makes it much harder to spend!

THERE'S NO SUCH THING AS A ONE-SIZE-FITS-ALL BUDGET.

It's easier said than done, I know, but smart spending will lead to smart shopping. And over the course of the next six chapters, I'm going to help you become the smartest and most stylish shopper you know.

Work the Web

Try these websites to help with your budgeting:

Mint.com

LearnVest.com

Geezeo.com

BudgetTracker.com

Buxfer.com

A
Chapter 2

ROAD MAP
TO STYLE

I've always been the kind of woman who knows exactly what she wants. I knew by age thirteen that I wanted to work in fashion. I knew within a few weeks of meeting my husband that I wanted to marry him. And when I moved to Philadelphia, I looked at only one apartment before declaring it "the one." The only place where I haven't been so decisive through the years? My style.

In photos of myself as a little girl, I was always in a dress and my accessory of choice—oversize bows. When I got older, I didn't have many opportunities to flex my fashion muscles, since I wore a uniform to school and spent my weekends on the sidelines in a cheerleading uniform. Still, I would spend hours poring over fashion magazines and dreaming of the day when I could wear "real clothes." When I did get a chance to dress myself, my tastes shifted from preppy turtlenecks and blazers in my early teens (the Limited Too had just opened) to grunge in my later teens, when Nirvana and Pearl Jam dictated not only music trends but fashion ones as well. At one point, I actually made my mom buy me a pair of Dr. Martens.

As I got ready to leave for college in Washington, D.C., I was excited to shed my school uniform and try out new styles. I would define my college style as experimental—I played around with trends that I probably had no business wearing but wanted to try simply because celebrities were wearing them at the time: tube tops, halter tops, endless black pants, and chunky platforms. But hey, I was in my early twenties, and that's the best time to experiment to extremes—you have gravity and youth on your side! Besides, if Victoria Beckham—now one of the world's best-dressed women, in my opinion—rocked a tube top during her Spice Girls days, I'm allowed to have dabbled with them, too!

After college, I adopted a feminine and flirty style that has remained more or less a constant ever since. I found that shorter hemlines and soft, romantic tones look best on me. I don't think I even owned a pair of black shoes until a few years ago—and for a girl living in New York City, that wasn't easy!

By my late twenties, I knew what I liked, but as a petite woman, I always felt my choices were limited. I quickly learned that I could shop off the rack if I became best friends with my tailor—and I did! I still visit her weekly, and she tells me constantly that I'm her best client.

Now, at thirty-three, I have a strong command of what looks best on my body and what makes me feel the most confident. Rest assured, though, it took me a while to get to this point, because style isn't born overnight. Your fashion sense will change over time based on your size, your age, your mood, and, of course, ever-changing fashion trends that even the best of us fall victim to. But even as your taste evolves, the basic principles of style remain constant, so you'll be able to use the knowledge you learn in this book no matter what phase of your life you're in.

DEVELOPING YOUR PERSONAL STYLE

W hy is it so important to develop your own personal style? Not only because it tells people about who you are without your having to say a word, but also because it will save you time and money (not to mention embarrassment) in the long run. If you don't know what you like or what looks best on your body, when you get inside a store, you'll be easily swayed by what's on the mannequins.

If you haven't identified your style, your closet will be filled with extraneous or unflattering clothes that you don't like and don't wear, which is a waste of your hard-earned cash and your closet space. If you spend some time determining what looks good on your body type and what suits your lifestyle, you can be sure that every piece in your wardrobe makes sense for you.

Jennifer Aniston is a perfect example of someone with a very specific, well-defined personal style. Go back ten years and you'll see that while her hair, makeup, and love interests may have changed, her red-carpet uniform has pretty much stayed the same: black, short, and well tailored. The woman knows what works for her, and she works it in return.

On the other hand, you might be more like Madonna, your tastes constantly evolving like a chameleon. Just as your taste buds change over time, your style might shift as the years go by—and that's why it's called *personal* style.

If you're not sure what image you want to convey, however, that's OK! Following is a fun, easy quiz that will help you on your way to finding your sense of style.

Think Chic

Mannequins are long, lean, and constructed with perfect proportions; they have no cellulite to camouflage or muffin tops to disguise. They are not your friend—and the way clothes look on display in no way reflects how they will look on you! For this reason, it's crucial that you try everything on—no exceptions!

IDENTIFYING YOUR STYLE

1. At the nail salon, you usually go for:

a. the hottest color of the season

b. something nude and neutral

c. red, always red

d. Lilly Pulitzer pink

e. fuchsias and bright hues

f. something unexpected, like blues and greens

2. When shopping, you're usually drawn to:

a. anything you spotted on the runway or red carpet

b. A-lines, sleek sheaths, and slim black trousers

c. fitted silhouettes and cuts that show off your curves in attention-getting colors

d. cashmere cable knits, crisp khakis, and tailored blazers in neutral tones

e. soft colors and styles with ladylike details

f. loose dresses or skirts and colorful prints

3. Which of the following best describes your home décor?

a. Streamlined and tonal with rich textures

b. Minimal yet warm, with lots of neutral tones and clean lines

c. Fun and colorful with touches of glam accessories and lots of mirrors

d. Comfortable and traditional

e. Shabby chic

f. Lots of textiles, earth tones, and items you picked up on your world travels

4. Of these women, the one whose style you most admire is:

a. Sarah Jessica Parker

b. Jacqueline Kennedy

c. Kim Kardashian

d. Reese Witherspoon

e. Elizabeth Taylor

f. Kate Hudson

5. When you wear a pattern, it's usually:

a. bold color blocking

b. none; patterns aren't really my thing

c. graphic, like polka dots and chevron

d. traditional yet colorful, like stripes and plaids

e. delicate and sophisticated

f. unique or ethnic, like ikat or tie-dye

6. Your favorite shoe is:

a. this fall's must-have ankle boot

b. a classic leather pump

c. red patent stilettos

d. comfy but stylish flats

e. peep-toe pumps

f. flat gladiator sandals

7. What is your dream office ensemble?

a. Sleek trousers and a leather jacket with booties

b. Tailored pants and a sweater with flats

c. A blouse and a colorful pencil skirt with heels

d. Dark jeans and a button-down with loafers

e. A wrap dress with pumps

f. A flowy skirt with a tee and sandals

8. If you could splurge on one designer bag, it would be a:

a. Proenza Schouler PS 1

b. Tod's satchel

c. Balenciaga motorcycle bag

d. Goyard tote bag

e. Chanel flap bag

f. Vintage cross-body satchel

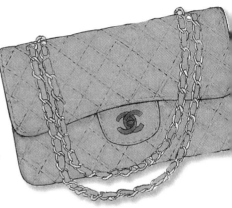

9. What would you wear to a cocktail party?

a. Slinky minidress

b. Perfect-fitting LBD

c. Bandage dress

d. Colorful and/or printed sheath dress

e. Flirty A-line dress

f. Crochet dress

10. If we opened your closet, what color palette would we mostly see?

a. Black with touches of bold, electric color

b. Neutrals like navy, charcoal, camel, and beige

c. Stand-out colors like red and fuchsia mixed with rich jewel tones

d. Navy, khaki, white, and touches of pinks

e. Soft blushes and creams with pops of brights

f. Earth tones like forest green, tan, chocolate, and rust

[RESULTS]

If you answered mostly A's,
YOU'RE A RISK TAKER.

You live for fashion and aren't scared to try out the latest trend. Your wardrobe is full of runway-inspired buys that make you feel like you just stepped out of the pages of *Vogue*. You know how to spot a hot trend, but you may not always know how to make it work for you.

Celebrity Style Icons: Cameron Diaz, Blake Lively, Sarah Jessica Parker

If you answered mostly B's,
YOU'RE A MINIMALIST.

Your closet is full of clothes that are timeless and elegant. You'd rather look put together than styled, and you lean toward neutrals or black when it comes to colors. While your closet is filled with sleek and tailored silhouettes, you'd love to find a new way to add some spice to your looks.

Celebrity Style Icons: Jennifer Aniston, Nicole Kidman, Sandra Bullock

If you answered mostly C's,
YOU'RE A SHOWSTOPPER.

When you walk into a room, everyone notices. Your fashion choices are bold and your clothes are characterized by slim cuts and figure-hugging silhouettes that showcase your curves. You're attracted to clothes that attract attention, but you'd also like to learn how to add some class to your sass!

Celebrity Style Icons: Sofía Vergara, Kim Kardashian, Halle Berry

If you answered mostly D's,
YOU'RE A GIRL NEXT DOOR.

You've never met a cable-knit cardigan you didn't like. Clothes in preppy colors and relaxed fits are your closet staples, and you tend to shop more for traditional pieces than for seasonal trends. Your wardrobe hasn't changed much since college, but you're open to updating your style with a few more fashion-forward items.

Celebrity Style Icons: Reese Witherspoon, Taylor Swift

If you answered mostly E's,
YOU'RE A ROMANTIC.

When it comes to fashion, you want to feel like a lady first and a trendsetter second. Your preferred color palette is full of neutrals like blush, pink, and beige, and your clothes have a soft, girly quality about them. You prefer cuts that skim your curves and that show off your figure in a sophisticated way, but you could stand to edge things up a bit.

Celebrity Style Icons: Eva Longoria, Leighton Meester, Salma Hayek

If you answered mostly F's,
YOU'RE A HIPPIE CHIC.

Your style is characterized by a carefree approach to fashion. You love floaty, dreamy clothes in earth tones that incorporate vivid patterns like ikat and tie-dye and have a hint of the 1970s. Your look is laid-back, and you're much happier shopping in a vintage store than in your local mall. While you live for easy, effortless clothes, you wouldn't mind adding a few chic outfits to your wardrobe.

Celebrity Style Icons: Nicole Richie, Kate Hudson, Rachael Zoe

[ ]

Finding Inspiration

If I had a nickel for every time people are flat-out shocked when I tell them where some piece of my outfit is from, I'd be a millionaire. They can't believe I got my to-die-for motorcycle jacket in the kids' department at Old Navy because when I wear it, it looks like it came off the Balenciaga runway. And while I'd love to take *all* the credit, part of the credit has to go to my "sources." Now, when I say "sources," I'm not talking about top-secret Central Intelligence Agency operatives (or Fashion Institute of Technology operatives, for that matter). I simply mean the people, places, and publications that get my creative juices flowing. Inspiration can come from anywhere: a girl you see walking down the street, a style blog, an advertisement, or even something seemingly unrelated to fashion.

I have a weakness, for example, for great interior design. One of my favorite people in the industry is noted interior designer Kelly Wearstler. She has an unbelievable knack for mixing prints; her design aesthetic is totally unexpected—and the way she dresses isn't bad, either! One day I came across an article about one of her hotel projects, and I immediately tore it out and stuck it on my bulletin board. I loved the colors and patterns she incorporated into the room, so I used those images as my inspiration for future shopping trips and

Style Cents

Keep a vision board at home and hang things on it that inspire you to dress with pizzazz. It could be anything: a page torn from a magazine, a piece of fabric or ribbon, a paint swatch, or a photo from a day when you thought you looked phenomenal. If you want something you can take with you on the go, fill a binder with clear page protectors and slip your inspiration pieces inside. Pinterest accomplishes the same task quickly, easily, and clutter-free for those who are tech savvy (or neat freaks)!

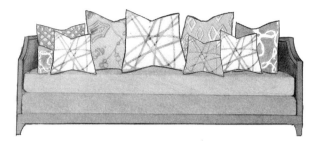

[YOU'RE NOT GOING TO FIND JUST THE
RIGHT OUTFIT FOR TAKING YOUR DAUGHTER'S
GIRL SCOUT TROOP TO THE BOTANICAL
GARDEN IN *W*!]

subsequent outfits. It pushed me outside of my comfort zone (which can be a very good thing), and it also helped me to focus my search so I wasn't left aimlessly wandering the aisles.

Some of my favorite places to find inspiration are, predictably, fashion magazines. But fashionistas in training, take note: I'm not talking about *Vogue* or *W* or some obscure Japanese publication. While there's nothing wrong with looking at those magazines for fun, they don't really do much in the form of usable inspiration, nor do they give you concrete ideas for putting together outfits that work for your own life. As real women, we have real needs when it comes to style. Trust me, you're not going to find just the right outfit for taking your daughter's Girl Scout troop to the botanical garden in *W*! Keeping that in mind, some of my favorite magazines for outfit inspiration are more accessible publications like *O, The Oprah Magazine*; *Lucky*; *Marie Claire*; and *Glamour*. While these titles still do an amazing job of scouting the latest trends, they do it in a way that makes sense for those of us who aren't runway models.

When I get my monthly mags, I take some time to go through each one. I really encourage you to do this, too—and not while you're doing a million other things or your kids are pulling at your pant legs. You need to be focused on *you,* not your to-do list. I promise that if you give yourself the time and space to think and question the fashion that you see in front of you, your style will slowly start to reveal itself, so give yourself the luxury of a few hours here and there for research.

Now, I know the moms and busy career women out there are probably scoffing at such a suggestion. I understand that it seems frivolous to be worrying about fashion when you've got lunches to pack or presentations to prepare, but trust me, this is not a wasted exercise! Every woman deserves the opportunity to be happy with the way she looks. How you feel about yourself will carry over into your overall demeanor and the way you treat your coworkers, friends, and family. Neglecting your appearance will do nothing but bury your self-confidence and make you resentful for all that you've sacrificed. Dedicate just a few hours a week to your self-betterment, and the return on your investment will be huge. You'll feel more capable, more confident, and sexier too!

Haute Hint

Sign up for subscriptions of your favorite magazines—you can save 70 percent or more than if you bought them on the newsstand. Or have all your friends subscribe to different publications and then trade with one another. You can make photocopies of the pages that you like or don't like rather than tearing them out.

As you go through the pages of each magazine, look at everything—some of the best inspiration can come from the advertisements rather than the editorial. If you see something that you respond to, don't question it—just tear it out and put it to the side. You want to be sure that you look at items individually; while you may not love the whole look, you may really like one piece. If you see something you absolutely hate, make sure to tear that item out too. It's just as important to learn what you *don't* like as what you *do* like. Repeat this as you go through each title and see what you end up with. You may have a pile of pages that looks like a Rubik's cube of fashion, or you could find that you tore out the same kinds of items or styles over and over again. Both outcomes are equally important.

This "tear-outs" exercise can be repeated with fashion websites and blogs. Simply print out the pictures you respond to or bookmark them on a website like Pinterest.com. There are so many resources online for finding inspiration, and here's my favorite part about them: They're free! When you're searching for these blogs online, use keywords like "personal style blog" or "daily outfit posts." This type of blog features authors who post daily or almost-daily pictures of themselves in head-to-toe outfits, which means you'll get plenty of ideas that you can put to work in your own closet, hopefully inspiring you to be bolder than you normally would be with your fashion choices. And don't be scared if their style is a far cry from how you dress daily—it's all about giving yourself freedom and flexibility to interpret trends in a way that works for *you*.

Online Inspiration Guide

In addition to magazines, there are a number of great resources out there that can inform your style and give you ideas for how you can be a better dresser. When I need creative stimulation, here's where I turn:

Blogs. No matter your sensibilities, there's a blog to meet your needs. Of course, I recommend my own, CheapChicas.com, but some of my other favorites include:

Late Afternoon (www.lateafternoonblog.com). When you're in the mood to just browse through beautiful photos in hopes that the effect will rub off on you, look no further than this blog.

Extra Petite (www.extrapetite.com). Though women of all shapes and sizes can glean ideas from this site, petite women in particular will love this blog, which is packed full of outfit ideas, tailoring hints, and more.

The Cut (www.nymag.com/thecut). The Cut is *New York* magazine's site dedicated to all things fashion and beauty.

Wendy's Lookbook (www.wendyslookbook.com). You'll be wowed by how Wendy Nguyen injects glamour into her day-to-day life—and inspires to do the same.

Atlantic-Pacific (www.atlantic-pacific.blogspot.com). The mix of looks displayed here bounces between demure and sophisticated one day and vibrant and eclectic the next. If Carrie Bradshaw had a style blog, I imagine this is what it would look like.

Song of Style (www.songofstyle.blogspot.com). When you see how many effortlessly adorable looks this blogger puts together each week, you'll feel too guilty to let your style slip.

Calivintage (www.calivintage.com). This site encompasses hipster fashion at its finest.

The Glamourai (www.theglamourai.com). Part outfit inspiration blog, part fashion editorial site, part photo diary, this site is always full of pretty pictures and is definitely never dull.

Where Did U Get That (www.wheredidugetthat.com). Blogger Karen shows off not only her own fabulously funky outfits but also those of people she runs into on the street.

Who What Wear (www.whowhatwear.com). This all-encompassing fashion site examines celebrity style, monitors trends, and dissects runway collections.

The Ray and the Ro (www.therayandthero.com). Namesake bloggers Rachel and Roberta prefer to let the pictures do the talking, offering minimal bits of advice and commentary while rounding up essential items, must-have trends, fashion news, and steals.

On the Racks (www.ontheracks.com). This site offers wearable looks for the young city dweller.

Lookbooks. Whenever I'm in a style slump, or I'm just not sure how to wear something, I venture on over to sites like ShopBop.com, HM.com, and LuLus.com, which compile covetable head-to-toe looks that you can attain with just a click! Best of all, they get updated multiple times a month so you don't have to wait four weeks for the next issue.

Online catalogs. If you're not a regular customer or just prefer to be green, you might not receive store catalogs in the mail. But catalogs do more than just clog up your mailbox—they can actually help you see how to put pieces together. Not to fear, though: Many stores offer their catalogs for perusal on their websites.

Online magazines. Not all style mags are sold on newsstands. These free web-only e-zines include articles, interviews, news briefs, fashion shoots, and more! Check out the following for a more thorough perspective on what's happening in fashion:

The Edit, Net-A-Porter's magazine (www.net-a-porter.com/magazine)

Fashion Q and A (www.fashionqanda.co.uk)

Iconique (www.iconique.com)

T, the *New York Times* style magazine (www.nytimes.com/pages/t-magazine)

Fashion156 (www.fashion156.com)

Hint (www.hintmag.com)

Pinterest. See what friends and fashion icons are loving by logging on to this virtual bulletin board. Here are a few of my favorite pinners to follow:

Design Seeds (www.pinterest.com/designseeds). Peek inside the brain of Jessica Colaluca, who draws color inspiration from unexpected places. Visiting her Pinterest page is always a trip down a rabbit hole for me in the best and most colorful way!

Glitter Guide (www.pinterest.com/glitterguide). The people behind TheGlitterGuide.com know sometimes you just need an injection of something girly in your life. Count on them for sparkly, shiny things.

Style Me Pretty (www.pinterest.com/stylemepretty). I may have gotten married five years ago, but that doesn't mean I can't plan a vow renewal! You never have to stop dreaming of the perfect nuptials, thanks to this page filled with—OK, we'll say it—pure wedding porn!

Chad Syme (www.pinterest.com/chadsyme). Designer and photographer Chad Syme makes me think bigger and better for all my design projects—whether he's introducing me to a new font or giving love to an incredible logo.

Joy Cho (www.pinterest.com/ohjoy). Joy is not only a wonderful person (and a really good tennis player—we met taking lessons!), but she's just about one of the most stylish women I've ever met. When I'm looking for a smorgasbord of style, hers are my go-to boards!

The Beauty Department (www.pinterest.com/tbdofficial). Here you can find the very best in beauty (along with craft how-tos and gift ideas) from one of my favorite former reality-TV starlets, Lauren Conrad.

Stephanie Brinkerhoff (www.pinterest.com/stephanieannb). Fashion and beauty go hand in hand, so step up your hair and makeup game on this page curated by professional hair stylist Stephanie Brinkerhoff.

Jessica Comingre (www.pinterest.com/jessicacomingre). This L.A.-based blogger and graphic designer's page is everything I love about laid-back West Coast style.

Once you have your tear-outs, start making piles. The pages that you *don't* like go in one pile and will serve as a guide for what you won't be buying and what you'll be removing from your closet later on. The pages that you *do* like will go into a pile that will then be sorted by category.

Create as many categories as you need to feel organized, but the ones everyone should have are:

- Colors
- Prints
- Head-to-toe looks (These will also be really important when we get to our shopping trip in Chapter 4!)
- Accessories
- Unique items
- Love it . . . but don't know why

As you start to go through your tear-outs, you might realize that you've picked out similar looks from multiple magazines. Believe it or not, this is a great thing! There's something about that eggplant color or those platform-style shoes that really catches your eye, and now you have some direction for what you'll want to focus your style on. The perfect look for you may be seventies boho chic, when all this time you've been dressing more conservatively.

Looking at the cut and the shape of the items you picked out is also very important. Some of us like things cut close to the body, others prefer silhouettes with more volume, and some like both! Some of us dare to bare, while others prefer to stay buttoned-up. There's nothing wrong with either preference—your style is what makes you, you.

If you're responding to an article of clothing, a handbag, or a pair of shoes but you're not entirely sure why, it's important to ask yourself some questions to help you nail down exactly what it

Haute Hint

See something on a celebrity that you absolutely love? Some magazines will track down where a star got a certain item and—gulp—what the price is. (Some will kindly suggest similar look-for-less prices, too.) Don't see this? Try writing in via e-mail or tweeting them!

Think Chic

Within the last three months, recall what you were wearing at a time you felt . . .

sexy

powerful

romantic

flirty

professional

sophisticated

demure

Make note of how different clothes make you feel so they can be your go-to garments when you're looking for a little mood lift.

is that you like about that item. Here are some example questions to get you started:

Q: Why do I like the hemline of this skirt?
A: Because it's short and I love my legs.

Q: Why do I prefer a cotton sweater to a silk blouse?
A: Because my kids stain everything and cotton's so much easier to take care of.

Q: Why do I like the way I feel in cropped pants?
A: Because I'm petite and they make me feel taller.

By taking the time to ask personal style questions, you'll be able to really pick up on the small details that will help you create a wardrobe that you love and—if you're really being honest—one that's functional, too. The reason most of us end up with "a closet full of clothes, but nothing to wear" is because we're buying just to buy; we're not shopping for things that suit our lifestyle. In order to shop smarter, you need to take a long, hard look at your day-to-day life and assess what types of activities you regularly participate in. Are you an event planner who's constantly attending swanky soirees? Or are you a stay-at-home mom for whom the most glamorous event on your iPhone calendar is your neighbor's kid's birthday party? There's no right or wrong answer—this isn't intended to make you feel bad about your social life (or lack thereof). It's simply to help you make truthful, realistic fashion choices that fit your life and to help you home in on items that will inspire you to get dressed with a little more purpose in the morning. Even if you're just running to the grocery store to buy more baby formula, putting on a cute pair of pants and a blouse is just as easy as putting on your husband's college T-shirt and a pair of sweatpants—but the results are very different.

Haute Hint

Keep track of your daily activities in a day planner or in the calendar app on your phone. After a month, look back and take note of what types of extracurriculars and events you're regularly taking part in. This will help you honestly address your lifestyle-based fashion requirements.

Dos and Don'ts of Finding Your Style

DO set private time aside to go through your monthly magazines.

DON'T look at them while trying to cook dinner or at your son's soccer game—you'll get distracted and won't take enough away from the exercise.

DO go through each magazine page by page—even if it's *InStyle*'s as-thick-as-a-phonebook September issue!

DON'T just flip through—often the advertisements can provide just as much inspiration as an editorial spread, and you might miss something.

DO go with your gut, tearing out whatever strikes your fancy.

DON'T tear out simply what you know to be in style at the moment. Your style is what you want it to be, not what the Milan runways say it should be.

While this process may seem time-consuming and overwhelming at first, keep in mind that this evolution isn't supposed to happen overnight. It probably took you years to get into your style rut, so now you just need some patience and a swift kick in the butt—courtesy of me—to help you get out!

· ● ·

CELEBRITY
STYLE FILES

One of my favorite things to do every Wednesday is load up on the gossip magazines. And no, it's not because I want to know who George Clooney's dating this month—well, at least not *entirely* because of that. It's also because these celebrity weeklies come loaded with some of the best fashion advice $3.99 can buy.

See, most celebrities work with a personal stylist, someone who will make sure they're always dressed in the hottest looks. You're probably thinking, *That's great for them, but how does it help me?* Think about it: Most of these professionally styled looks get photographed by a fleet of

[
WE ALL LIKE TO THINK WE LOOK
LIKE JULIA ROBERTS IN THE RIGHT LIGHT.
]

paparazzi on a daily basis and end up all over the pages of the tabloids each week. And that's when it becomes free style advice for you. When Diane Kruger attends a luncheon in a neon blue dress with yellow shoes, that's because someone in the know told her to. Take this cue to incorporate similar looks into your day-to-day wardrobe.

But before you can completely copy a star's style, you first need to identify your celebrity twin—and yes, everyone has one! I'm not talking about whom you actually resemble, even though we all like to think we

My list of the best-dressed women in Hollywood is always evolving (much like my own personal style). And while the women in the following list have certainly made a mistake or two (who hasn't?), they've got way more wins than losses on their style scorecard.

1. **Cameron Diaz:** She's a total trendsetter. I love her bold, devil-may-care attitude with clothes.

2. **Olivia Palermo:** She's girly with an edge, which happens to be my favorite style combination.

3. **Emma Stone:** She's playful with her fashion in a way that could get

(continued)

look like Julia Roberts in the right light. No, I'm talking about finding someone with a similar body type—someone whose shape, height, and proportions are similar to your own. Be on the lookout for celebrities with your dimensions when you're flipping through your favorite magazines.

To illustrate the importance of finding the right celebrity twin, let's talk about Cameron Diaz for a moment. I adore her style, plain and simple. She can do no wrong in my eyes. She's the kind of girl you want to hate, but how can you? She (with the help of her stylist, of course) chooses clothes that show off her body in the most perfect way. Her body is long, lean, and athletic. The problem is, while I may love everything she wears, my body is the exact opposite of hers: I'm short and much more compact, and I just don't have the overall muscle tone she has. And while I can probably make some of the pieces she wears work for my body (with a little help from my tailor and a trainer), I can't just imitate her head-to-toe looks without looking like a frumpy elf. I'm likely much better off looking to someone more petite and with softer curves, like Rachel Bilson or Eva Longoria.

The goal is to find a celebrity who has proportions similar to yours so that you can literally steal her style! When you find your twin, study what she wears, how she wears it, and where she wears it, and then think of her style as a blueprint for your own look. If you watch closely, you'll see that celebrities never veer too far off their style track. After all, no one wants to end up on a worst-dressed list.

JUST YOUR TYPE

The first step in finding your celebrity twin is to determine your body type. In this section I've outlined five basic body types and given you goals for what you'll want to accomplish with your clothes, a list of celebrities with the same shape, tips for how to best dress yourself, and a few key pieces you should have in your closet.

Pear

- **DESCRIPTION:** Rounded hips and bottom wider than your shoulders; defined waistline; bust and stomach often flat

- **YOUR GOAL:** Downplay hips by showing off your arms and adding oomph to your chest

her in trouble, but her confidence helps her pull off any look.

4. **Gwyneth Paltrow:** She's just beyond words for me—she's classic but cool, sexy yet understated and purely effortless. If I could swap styles (and bodies!) with anyone, it would be Gwyneth.

5. **Catherine, the Duchess of Cambridge (aka Kate Middleton):** Kate shows how to do prim and proper with style.

6. **Lauren Conrad:** She's an everygirl. Her style feels totally accessible but still inspirational.

- **CELEBRITY BODY-TYPE TWINS:** Beyoncé, Jennifer Lopez, Eva Mendes, Rihanna

- **TIPS:**
  - Wear darker bottoms and lighter tops to emphasize your waist-line and minimize your curves down low.
  - Pair V-neck blouses with wide-leg pants or an A-line skirt to create an hourglass shape.
  - Choose forgiving jackets that are fitted through the bust and waist but gently flare over the hips.

- **KEY PIECES:**
  - A-line skirts with vertical-panel seaming
  - Shift dresses with a belt detail
  - Bold accessories that draw attention away from your lower half

Hourglass

- **DESCRIPTION:** Full bust and bottom with a narrow waist

- **YOUR GOAL:** Accentuate your curves without being overly sexy

- **CELEBRITY BODY-TYPE TWINS:** Kim Kardashian, Jennifer Hudson, Christina Hendricks, Sofía Vergara, Scarlett Johansson, Salma Hayek

- **TIPS:**
  - Avoid styles such as shifts or trapeze dresses that hide your small waist.

- Opt for V-neck or scoop necklines—both styles slim the neck and chest area and make you appear smaller.
- Choose a monochromatic outfit with a wide belt to slim your figure and balance your body.

- **KEY PIECES:**
  - Riding jackets and longer blazers with nipped waists
  - Midrise jeans
  - Dresses with color-blocked curves
  - Wrap-style coats

Athletic

- **DESCRIPTION:** Toned physique with few curves; straight from the shoulders through the waist and hips; sometimes referred to as "boyish" or "rectangular"

- **YOUR GOAL:** Create curves by mimicking a narrow waist and adding volume to the bust and hips

- **CELEBRITY BODY-TYPE TWINS:** Cameron Diaz, Jessica Alba, Keira Knightley, Gwyneth Paltrow, Kate Hudson, Jessica Biel

- **TIPS:**
  - Add femininity to your look with ruffle details or jeweled embellishments.
  - Avoid boxy cuts on top, which will only emphasize your straight shape.
  - Go for a straight or slim boot-cut jean instead of a skinny style.

- **KEY PIECES:**
  - Wrap dresses
  - Pencil skirts
  - Anything with a peplum to help add curves

Full-Figured

- **DESCRIPTION:** Rounded all over with little definition at the waist

- **YOUR GOAL:** Show off your curves and best assets without hiding your body

- **CELEBRITY BODY-TYPE TWINS:** Adele, Queen Latifah, Melissa McCarthy, Octavia Spencer, Rebel Wilson

- **TIPS:**
  - Invest in great shapewear: It gives you the best foundation for your clothes.
  - "The baggier, the better" is a myth—instead, buy clothes that skim your figure.
  - While dark colors are slimming, don't limit yourself to only black, which can get boring. Saturated colors can be just as slimming.

- **KEY PIECES:**
  - Anything with strategic ruching to help camouflage problem areas
  - Wide-leg pants
  - A-line skirts

Petite

- **DESCRIPTION:** Small stature (five-foot-four and under)

- **YOUR GOALS:** Lengthen the body and find clothes that don't drown you—or else tailor them so they don't

- **CELEBRITY BODY-TYPE TWINS:** Eva Longoria, Nicole Richie, Kelly Ripa, Kristin Chenoweth, Rachel Bilson, Hayden Panettiere

- **TIPS:**
  - Spend the money to hem pants and sleeves so that you don't look like a kid in her mom's clothes.
  - Wear shoes that make your legs appear longer to give the illusion of height. Opt for nude pumps over dark ankle-strap heels, which cut off your leg at the foot and instantly make you seem shorter.
  - Look for petite sizes when possible—not only will the lengths work better for you, but the overall fit and proportions will be better suited to your size as well. (And bear in mind that those elements are harder to achieve with alterations.)

- **KEY PIECES:**
  - Miniskirt or minidress
  - Skinny jeans
  - Cropped blazers

Haute Hint

While it can be a challenge to find specialty sizes, petite and plus-size women need not fear, as there are some size-minded retailers out there who cater to your needs.

PLUS SIZES

Big-Box Stores

- Target
- Walmart
- Kmart

For Up-to-the-Minute Trends

- ASOS.com's Curve brand
- Fashion to Figure stores

For Formal Wear

- David Meister
- Tadashi Shoji

For Everything

- Eloquii.com
- OneStopPlus.com

For Denim

- Paige Premium Denim
- James Jeans
- NYDJ
- CJ By Cookie Johnson

For Bridal

- Reem Acra
- White by Vera Wang

PETITES

For Up-to-the-Minute Trends

- ASOS.com
- Topshop

For Formal Wear

- Maggy London
- Calvin Klein
- Laundry by Shelli Segal
- Adrianna Papell

For Everything

- LOFT
- Banana Republic
- JCrew.com

For Denim

- Joe's Jeans
- AG Adriano Goldschmied

[ ]

If you've got a bootylicious figure like Beyoncé, but her style is a little more blinged out than you'd like, that's OK—I'm simply recommending that you copy the cuts of clothing that she wears, paying attention to where clothes hit her on her body and which parts she tends to show off. If you prefer a more vintage, romantic style—something like Taylor Swift's—there's no reason you can't adapt that to your body type. Or just because you've got a bombshell body like Sofía Vergara's doesn't mean you have to rock the va-va-voom ensembles she does. Just notice that she skips shapeless bag dresses in favor of form-fitting clothes that emphasize her tiny waist to avoid looking larger than she really is.

STYLE BY CHOICE

In my opinion, there are no rules when it comes to fashion. If you feel like dressing up for coffee in leather pants and six-inch YSL Tributes, more power to you! I have a feeling, though, that those "I'm having a fashion moment!" experiences are few and far between for the majority of us. On most days, you're just happy to walk out of the house looking like the best version of yourself in clothes that fit, look chic, and make you feel good. With that in mind, there are some *guidelines*—which, mind you, aren't the same as rules!—that can help you look your absolute best.

Sometimes we shop for the life we wish

we had, and while a fun, out-of-character purchase every once in a while is fine, part of looking your best is being honest about your body, your age, your geography, and your lifestyle. If you love shopping for party dresses but you live in a small town and have three kids under the age of five, your shopping and your lifestyle don't match. By honestly evaluating your day-to-day life *and* its limits, you'll make smarter choices about how to spend your money, which will help you decide what kinds of clothes deserve a precious place in your closet.

Here are some things to consider:

Age

No one wants to admit that they're too old to wear something, but the truth is, most of us are too old for *something*. I know, I know: Age is nothing but a number, but our style has to evolve as we get older whether we like it or not. Rather than dressing like you did as a teenager in an effort to look half your age (trust me—you're not fooling anyone), the better choice is to wear clothes that are appropriate for your age and make you look like the sharpest, smartest, most stylish woman of her generation, one who is completely comfortable with her place in life. *That* is the definition of being sexy in your own skin—*not* trying to shave twenty years off by cutting two inches off your hemline! That said, there are different guidelines, depending on your age group:

- **IN YOUR TWENTIES . . .** This is the time to really have fun with fashion! You're young enough to get away with almost anything, so think of this decade as a long tryout session when you can take the time and liberty to figure out what works and what doesn't without a lot of repercussions. Try every trend that strikes your fancy, but pay attention to how they look on you and take note of what works best for your body. Go fun and flirty with bright colors and animal prints. Try out a pair of parachute pants if the mood strikes you! And sky-high heels? Absolutely!

- **IN YOUR THIRTIES . . .** The things you can't wear aren't so much about colors or prints; the guidelines that apply now are more about cut and fit. While some women are blessed with legs that look gorgeous at any age, the mini you wear at thirty shouldn't be the same as the mini you wore when you were twenty. While there are plenty of miniskirts living in my closet today, they're not as tight as they once were, and I style them completely differently than I did a decade ago. Instead of wearing one with a fitted shirt, I'll now wear it with a loose-fitting, menswear-inspired button-down. The key here is balance. If you're going to show off a lot on the bottom, go covered up on top, and vice versa. Dress like the respectable, put-together young woman you are—old enough to have learned her lessons but young enough to still turn heads.

- **IN YOUR FORTIES AND FIFTIES . . .** Let your clothes reflect your maturity and opt for classic pieces rather than reaching for trends. Forget loud prints and bold hues—muted solids and simple, slimming patterns are your best friends. Remember, baggier clothes do not a mature woman make. Rather, opt for impeccably tailored pieces that show off your shape while maintaining a mature modesty. Switch to thicker heels with lower height. As for those skirts, you can still pull off a mini, but now you'll want to bring the hem down a bit and look for more elegant fabrics, such as wool, tweed, or bouclé. As you approach your fifties, swapping bare legs for a

[JUST BECAUSE YOU'RE GETTING OLDER DOESN'T MEAN YOU HAVE TO DRESS *OLD*.]

pair of textured tights might make the look more age appropriate. But remember, just because you're getting older doesn't mean you have to dress *old*—you just have to adapt your fashion choices and style to reflect a more grown-up version of you!

Geography

Where we live plays a large role in our style choices. Of course, temperature is a major factor. Is it usually cool at night but hot during the day where you are? If so, you'll want to buy items that look great layered. Do you live somewhere like Phoenix, where the only two seasons are hot and hotter? Then you probably have no need for a tweed blazer, no matter how adorable it might look in a catalog. In colder climates, invest in good-quality, eye-catching coats, since that's what people will see you in most of the time.

Of course, where you live involves more than just latitude and longitude. Are you a sky-rise-living city dweller or a slower-paced suburbanite? While I know that all suburbs are not created equal, for the most part, living in the burbs generally means a more relaxed approach to fashion. No one is going to give you dirty looks if you show up to a restaurant in leggings and flats, but they might if you waltz in wearing a sequin mini-dress and stilettos. On the other hand, show up underdressed to a trendy nightclub in Los Angeles, and you'll be turned away at the door. Consider the appropriateness of your attire for your setting.

Profession

It doesn't matter if you're a kindergarten teacher or a district attorney—the one thing we all have in common is that our work environment plays a key role in determining the kinds of clothes we buy. You probably spend five out of seven days a week in your workplace, which means that more than 70 percent of your wardrobe should be office appropriate.

That doesn't mean that you need to spend all your money on suits, but it does mean that you need to be conscious about your purchases to make sure you have enough clothes to get you through the week in style. If you spend Monday through Friday in a courtroom, you need professional clothes that err on the conservative side, such as suits, trousers, pencil skirts, and blouses. If you work as an art director at an advertising agency, you may be able to take more liberties with colors and cuts, but you still need to look professional for client meetings. For you, separates and prints will be key, allowing you to mix and match as the situation dictates. And if you're a busy mom, you need clothes that are functional above all else, but that doesn't mean they can't be fashionable too. Items like leggings and well-fitting jeans will look great with jersey tops, all of which can handle abuse from the kiddies and numerous washes.

X Factor

Style is a reflection of who you are as a person. It's the first thing people notice about you, and it's what they'll remember after you leave—be it good or bad. Clothes should be an outward statement of how you feel about yourself and a testament to your personality. So while the above considerations should play a large role in your clothing purchases, there are some things you'll want to buy that don't necessarily make sense. In moderation, that's not only OK—it's what makes your style uniquely yours. These things might not make sense on their own, but once they're incorporated into a wardrobe that fits your lifestyle, you'll see how they can give new life, energy, and personality to everything in your closet.

> STYLE IS THE FIRST THING PEOPLE NOTICE ABOUT YOU, AND IT'S WHAT THEY'LL REMEMBER AFTER YOU LEAVE—BE IT GOOD OR BAD.

Some of my favorite pieces in my wardrobe, for instance, are so impractical that even I don't understand the reason or motivation behind the purchase. But while these outliers, as I like to call them, may not live up to my practicality standards, they sure do liven up my wardrobe and make me feel great every time I wear them.

One of my favorite outliers is a sheer BCBG leopard-print blouse I bought on sale at Bloomingdale's for $75. I call it my Peg Bundy shirt. Now, normally, I'm not a super-body-conscious dresser, and even though my husband probably wishes I could bring some sexy back into my wardrobe, it's just not my usual style—and that's why this blouse is the perfect outlier for my closet. I've worn it out with leather leggings, with a full black skirt, and even with tailored brocade shorts. One time, on a particularly adventurous night, I even paired it with a black lace bra that just slightly peeked out through the material. What can I say? Sometimes a girl just needs a little sex appeal!

My other favorite outlier has a story, as all the best purchases do. I was in desperate need of new black pumps, and since I married a very smart

[SOMETIMES IMPRACTICAL CAN STILL BE AMAZING.]

man, he knew the fastest way to forgiveness after a particularly nasty fight was with a new pair of shoes! I am a true believer in buying quality over quantity if it's something that you wear all the time, and black pumps certainly fall into this category for me. Knowing this, my oh-so-brilliant husband brought home a pair of black sling-back Christian Louboutins that were *almost* perfect. Unfortunately, almost doesn't cut it when you're dropping a month's rent on shoes. So I did what any red-blooded, shoe-obsessed woman would do: I marched myself to the Louboutin store to exchange them for a classic Pigalle pump in black.

Or at least that's what I *intended* to do. Instead, I walked out of the store with a pair of cobalt-blue pumps with a silver platform. I have no excuse for this turn of events, other than to say that some things can't be explained with logic and reason. Yet to this day, my cobalt Louboutins put a smile on my face every time I wear them. It just goes to show that sometimes impractical can still be amazing.

The message I'm trying to get across to you is that you don't have to adhere completely to the fashion world's rules to curate your own style. If you're able to identify what you like and don't like, what types of clothes you respond to (even on other people), and what your lifestyle limitations are, you're well on your way to looking better than ever—and maybe, just maybe, to a pair of cobalt-blue pumps.

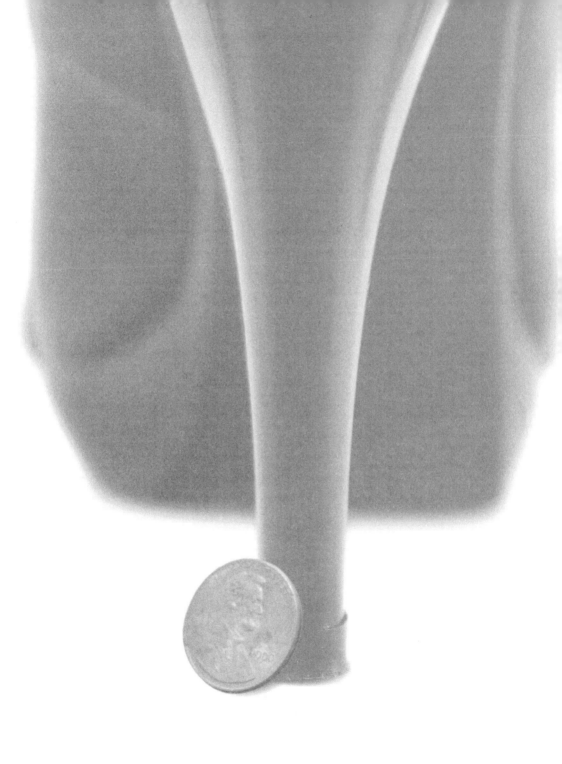

MAKING CENTS

Chapter 3

OF YOUR

CLOSET

U nlike a lot of men out there, my husband loves clothes. It was one of the things I found most attractive about him when we first met, and to this day, I love that he cares not only about how he looks, but about the way I look, too. He appreciates the effort I put into getting dressed, and he values my opinion on his sartorial choices. The only downside to my Prince Charming: He also needs his closet space!

Had I loved the man any less dearly, this could've been a deal breaker. But seeing that I kinda wanted him to stick around, I was forced to reach a compromise. After some intense negotiations, I got ownership of the closet and a small shoe wardrobe right outside our bedroom. My husband got the closet in our guest bedroom. And we share custody of a coat closet and a large IKEA wardrobe in our bedroom, which has been split in half and custom designed to our respective likings. Then, whatever is left (yes, there's still more) gets stored in every spare nook and cranny we've got, from beneath our bed to in unused kitchen cabinets.

If you're like me, and your closets—and cabinets, and crawl spaces—

are at capacity, the unfortunate truth is that there won't be anywhere to put any fabulous new purchases unless you clean out what you *don't* wear. What if I said you couldn't buy that new Tory Burch jacket until you threw out something you no longer love? You'd grab a trash bag faster than I can say Chanel! By getting rid of what you don't like or don't use, you're creating homes for better pieces that will encourage your most stylish self to shine.

By this point, you should have a good idea of your style and how to achieve it. Now it's time to see how what you already own fits into that picture, which items don't make sense for you anymore (or maybe never did), and which essential items you're still lacking. That's right: It's time to venture into your closet! *Bom bom bommmm . . .*

Luckily, braving your closet doesn't have to be like a scene in a scary movie. Sure, things might jump out at you here and there, and you might

BRAVING YOUR CLOSET DOESN'T HAVE
TO BE LIKE A SCENE IN A SCARY MOVIE.

see a few items that make you scream in horror (when did I ever think that a sparkly tube top was a good idea?!). But I'm going to tell you how to exorcise the demons of your wardrobe so the only devil in your life is the Prada-wearing one on your bookshelf.

Taking inventory of your closet is important for many reasons. First, organization is crucial to dressing your best. If you can't see what you have, you can't wear it. I don't know about you, but my mornings aren't like

[EXORCISE THE DEMONS OF YOUR WARDROBE SO THE ONLY DEVIL IN YOUR LIFE IS THE PRADA-WEARING ONE ON YOUR BOOKSHELF.]

leisurely paced Folgers commercials where I spend hours sipping coffee on a terrace. I'm lucky if I can remember to grab an apple for breakfast in my frantic rush to get to the train station for my daily commute to New York. But even on my most harried of mornings, my style doesn't suffer, and here's why: because I make it easy for myself to dress smartly.

It really irks me when I hear people say, "I just grabbed the first thing I saw," as a way to excuse their sloppy dressing. Why was that stained, mis-shapen sweater in your closet to begin with? I'm going to make it so that the first thing you'll grab will be something stylish that you feel confident in—as will the second thing and the third thing and the very last thing. Your closet should be easily "shoppable," the same way it's easy to spot pieces you love in your favorite store. You want the selection to be expertly curated, easily visible, nicely displayed, and ready to slip on at a moment's notice. With just a little prep work, the task of getting ready will become infinitely easier and faster.

There's also the simple matter of space. I know we all wish we had a closet like Mariah Carey's, but the reality is that most of us are working with a very limited amount of square footage. I don't have anywhere near

> THE FIRST THING YOU'LL GRAB WILL BE SOMETHING STYLISH THAT YOU FEEL CONFIDENT IN—AS WILL THE SECOND THING AND THE THIRD THING AND THE VERY LAST THING.

enough room in my closet for all my things. My husband likes to say I'm a borderline hoarder, but I prefer to think of myself as a *collector*. My lack of space combined with my penchant for holding on to things fuels my obsessive attitude toward organization. It's not a luxury in my case; it's an absolute necessity.

Out of the Closet

There are a lot of clever storage solutions to make the most of the unused spaces in your home. Here are a few I've discovered:

Under the bed. I know, not exactly groundbreaking. But beneath your five-hundred-thread-count sheets and your Tempur-Pedic mattress topper lies the most useful and accessible space for storage outside of your closet. Buy as many under-bed bins as will fit.

Kitchen cabinets. As I confessed earlier, if you were to open some of the cabinets in my kitchen, instead of cookware or canned goods, you'd find things like shoes and scarves. It may seem silly, but I shop more than I cook, and I have an excessive amount of kitchen storage, which would otherwise go unused. Just be sure to store anything you keep in the kitchen in protective boxes to prevent food and grease stains and smells.

Out-of-use suitcases. You tote your filled-to-the-brim Tumi around when you travel, so why have it sit empty on a shelf when you're homebound? And those vintage trunks you use as side tables? They're also perfect for storage. Whether functional or purely decorative, luggage makes for great bonus space. (And when you're ready to use that luggage for its intended purpose, turn to the photo insert for packing tips and wardrobe ideas for going on vacation.)

Behind the couch. If your sofa is along a wall and you have space to spare, pull it out six to twelve inches and slip skinny boxes behind it. Without anyone being the wiser, you just dramatically increased your storage space!

Cleaning out your closet may seem like a monumental task, but I'm here to help. Together, we're going to decide what to keep (and how to take care of those pieces) and what to do away with (and what you should do with those discards). In the end, you'll have gained some satisfaction, a little bit of sanity, and hopefully a renewed enthusiasm for style..

The Importance of Organizing

Cleaning out your closet can do wonders for your life. Just ask Amanda Kuzak, owner of Kuzak's Closet (www.kuzakscloset.com), a professional organizing business based in Silicon Valley, California. Since 2004, she's helped technology CEOs and area celebrities take control of their clutter and reclaim their closets.

Q: What is the most common problem people seem to have when it comes to organizing their closets?

A: Letting go—especially of items that they haven't worn in years but that they think will come back into style or that they'll eventually fit into again.

Q: Why do people form emotional attachments to their clothes?

A: So many of my clients associate their clothing with a particular event in their life and expect to replicate the same feeling whenever they wear it. I always have to remind them that just because they met their significant other wearing the patchwork sweater with shoulder pads from the early eighties doesn't mean they need to wear it (or store it) still today!

Q: What's the biggest hurdle to having a clean closet?

A: Sticking to a schedule! Many of my clients wait to edit their wardrobes until their closet and wardrobe have lost almost all functionality. By parting with things little by little—and adding things little by little—everything will stay in balance.

WHERE TO START

Twice a year—during the winter-to-spring and summer-to-fall seasonal transitions—I complete the purging process I'll outline in this chapter. It can undoubtedly be time-consuming, so set aside an entire day to dedicate yourself to it. I like to enlist the help of a friend to keep me on track and make a project that can feel like a chore turn into something fun! What's in it for her, you ask? Since I make sure to choose a friend who's about my size, she gets her pick of the clothes I clean out!

Begin with the no-brainers: Throw away any clothes that are irrevocably stained, faded, pitted out, or ripped beyond repair. Even the Salvation Army doesn't want those sad sacks.

If a garment gets shrunken or stained in the wash, all hope isn't necessarily lost. Try these remedies immediately, and you may be able to salvage the item. (If the damage was done a considerable amount of time ago, or you've already dried the stained item, you may still have to dump those duds.)

Shrunken sweaters: Soak the shrunken garment in a solution of tepid water and a tablespoon of baby shampoo (hair conditioner also works if you don't have baby shampoo handy) for fifteen minutes to loosen the fibers. Drain the sink, lightly pressing out some of the water from the garment. Then lay the sweater flat on a towel to dry, dabbing the item gently with another towel to remove excess water. Gently stretch the sweater to the desired shape and size, placing weighted objects around the edges to help it maintain its shape. Allow to dry.

Color bleed from another item: Remove the offending item from the wash and rewash the affected items with color-safe bleach or one cup of distilled white vinegar in addition to detergent. (You can spot-test the bleach if you're nervous about using it on the items in question.) If that doesn't work, pour an oxygen-based bleach (Clorox 2, OxiClean, or Tide Stain Release) in a bucket of water and soak the stained item for eight hours; repeat if needed. Wash and dry as normal.

Stains: Different types of stains require different treatments.

> **Red wine:** Immediately blot with white wine or club soda. If those aren't available, pour salt on the spot. When you get home, dab the spot with a solution of one part dish soap and two parts hydrogen peroxide (best to use on white or color-safe fabrics only).

Coffee: Run cold water through the back of the stained area. Treat the area on both sides with a mix of laundry detergent, cold water, and distilled white vinegar. Rinse. Pretreat with liquid detergent if the stain remains, and then launder.

Deodorant: White residue from your antiperspirant can be removed by rubbing the area with a clean sock, used dryer sheet, or stiff sponge. If the area is yellowed, try treating it with one of the following: a solution of equal parts ammonia and water; crushed aspirin tablets in water; a paste made of water and baking soda; lemon juice and salt; vinegar; or even unseasoned meat tenderizer.

Dirt: Wait until any wet mud has dried; then scrape off the dirt with a knife. Pretreat the area with a paste of liquid dish soap and powdered laundry detergent, and then wash as normal.

Next, find three large boxes or bins. Label one "Ditch," one "Keep," and one "Store." Try on every piece of clothing in your closet—and I mean *every single piece.* After reassessing your personal style in the last chapter, you never know how your opinion might've changed on a certain piece of clothing, or how your go-to holiday party frock is fitting after nearly a year has gone by. Remember, we're doing a little work *now* to take the

guesswork out of getting ready in the mornings *forever.* If you know—not just think—everything in your closet fits flawlessly, that's half the battle!

If you don't already have one, invest in a full-length mirror. As you try on each piece, study yourself in the mirror and honestly evaluate it. Does it fit? Does it flatter? Does it make you think, "Damn, I look good!" when you're wearing it? If the answer is no for any reason that isn't fixable (see page 106 for a list of what is and isn't), it goes in the first bin:

Ditch

It's time to get serious and say buh-bye to the superfluous items sucking up space in your closet.

What Should I Shed?

- **ANYTHING YOU HAVEN'T WORN IN A YEAR.** Here's an easy way to figure out which items have gone untouched: Hang all your hangers the wrong way (with the hook facing toward you). When you wear something and hang it back up, put the hanger on the rod the correct way. At the end of a year, whichever items are on hangers still facing out get the boot.

- **ANYTHING THAT DOESN'T FIT YOU ANYMORE.** Don't hang on to garments you've outgrown in the hope that one day you'll fit into them again (unless your body is undergoing a major metamorphosis, as with a serious diet or a pregnancy). A closet full of "skinny" clothes doesn't do you any good when you're not so skinny anymore. Hold on to clothes that fit you today—then, if you do drop those pesky ten pounds, you can reward yourself with some new clothes to celebrate (or take in the ones you were wearing before).

- **ANYTHING THAT ISN'T FLATTERING OR MAKES YOU FEEL ANYTHING BUT FABULOUS.** Remember all those magazine tear-outs you put in the "don't like" pile? If you spot something in your closet that matches one of those looks, get rid of it. You should love what you wear and love the way you look in it.

- **ANYTHING THAT WAS ONCE TRENDY BUT ISN'T ANYMORE.** Yes, what goes around comes around, but if you're holding on to that fringed jacket waiting for it to come back in style, you'll be waiting an awfully long time. Your closet should be a museum for your best finds, not a mausoleum for dead trends. Get rid of the has-beens now to make room for new trends (or at least *store* them; see page 111). I promise, you won't even know they're gone.

What Should I Do with the Discards?

There are lots of ways to turn your trash into someone else's treasure. Here are a few ideas to get you started:

- **SELL THEM TO A CONSIGNMENT SHOP.** Designer clothes or pieces from well-known stores can fetch a pretty penny at better consignment shops.

- **SELL THEM ONLINE.** What you can't sell on consignment can be sold online via sites like eBay or Etsy. Using a digital camera, take clear, close-up photos of each item. Write detailed, keyword-laden headlines and thorough descriptions of the piece you're selling. Once a garment has sold, be sure to ship it promptly.

The ABCs of Consignment

Working with consignment shops is a great way to get cash for your unwanted items without having to do all the work! While we'll talk about the best methods for *shopping* secondhand in Chapter 6, here's how to *sell* your items like a pro:

Call ahead to find out what the shop is currently in the market for. Some stores want only in-season or out-of-season goods, whereas others might want specific styles, brands, sizes, and so on.

To give yourself the best shot at making a deal, make sure the items have no stains or imperfections, and have your pieces laundered and ironed.

Choose a store that carries items similar in style to yours.

Make relationships at your go-to shop. When the staff knows your clothes sell well, they're more likely to accept items from you in the future. And working primarily with one shop will also cut down on your traveling time.

Ask to see the store's contracts and policies. Every store works differently, so find out what percentage of the sale price you get and how long they keep the items (usually thirty, sixty, or ninety days).

Pay attention to location. Stores in more upscale areas attract better buyers for your designer items, so drive the extra twenty minutes to get to the poshest parts of town.

No one said that what you consign has to have been *yours*. Yard sales are ripe with potential for cheap fashion finds that you can flip for ten times the price.

- **DONATE THEM.** Thrift shops like Goodwill and the Salvation Army will take your unwanted clothing as long as it's in decent shape. Some charity organizations will even pick up discards from your home. Be sure to keep a record of what you donate and get a tax receipt so you can write off the donation.

   For business attire, consider donating your goods to an organization like Dress for Success Worldwide or the Women's Alliance, which help struggling women find clothes for job interviews. Similarly, there are a number of organizations that accept formal dresses for underprivileged teenage girls who otherwise wouldn't have a dress for school dances. Donate My Dress (www.donatemydress.org) is a nationwide organization, or search online for one in your area.

- **HOST A CLOTHING SWAP.** Invite friends over to your place for a swap party! Have everyone bring items they no longer want, and be sure to invite people who wear similar sizes so no one's left out. Whatever's left at the end of the night gets donated to charity.

- **GIVE TO FRIENDS AND FAMILY.** Does your sister look great in blue? Give her the aqua blouse you were going to get rid of.

Secrets of the Stylists

Got a stubborn piece of clothing that doesn't do what it's supposed to? Try these tips to get misbehaving clothes in line before ditching them:

1. **Double-stick tape.** Prevent a Janet Jackson–style nip slip by securing draped or low-cut tops to your skin using one of a variety of fashion tapes available or good old-fashioned Scotch double-sided tape.

2. **Nipple covers.** Love that clingy top, but feel like you're always a little, uh, overexposed? Keep the high beams at bay with stick-on nipple covers that will bring the modesty back to a flimsy shirt.

3. **Shapewear.** Is your junk in the trunk looking a little lumpy under that hip-hugging dress? Don't trash the outfit; just invest in some seriously good shapewear, like Spanx. They'll smooth you out and keep your goods in place so clothes can fall better.

4. **Shoe insoles.** Before you send your uncomfortable boots walking, give your kicks an assist with gel pads, which can ease your discomfort. If a shoe is a half size too big, buy heel inserts from Hug

My Heels or Dr. Scholl's for Her, which also sells padded strips that you can cut into customized sizes thanks to its tape dispenser–like packaging. Apply those to the heel for added grip, or anywhere a shoe rubs you the wrong way, for a much more peaceful union.

5. Washers. Leave the hemline acrobatics to Marilyn Monroe. If a flouncy skirt gets dangerous in high winds, simply add washers or quarters to the hem of a skirt to weigh it down. Inserting them into the seam is the most foolproof method, but if you're a slouch with a needle and thread, you can glue them to the interior of the hemline.

Keep

There are three main categories of clothes that you should hang on to. They are:

1. Basics

Just as a well-built home has to start with a solid foundation, a well-constructed closet must be built on solid foundation pieces, too. These will be your basics—simple, timeless, classic pieces that never go out of style and can be mixed and matched with one another just as easily as they can go with busier, more complex items. If you invest wisely in these basics, they can—and should—last for a long time. And because they're a neutral color and a timeless shape, you can keep them year after year.

Back to Basics

Below is a checklist of basic items every woman should have, depending on where you live and your body type. As you'll learn more about in Chapter 5, these are garments worth investing in:

	HAVE	DON'T HAVE
TOPS:		
• Simple tank in both black and white		
• White button-down		
• Basic, stretchy cotton short-sleeve T-shirts in white, black, and gray **>>**		
• Basic, stretchy cotton long-sleeve T-shirts in white, black, and gray		
• Neutral-colored camisoles		
• Thin black turtleneck		
• Crew- or V-neck sweater in basic color		
• Heavy knit sweater **>>**		
• Cardigan		

PANTS:

• Black suiting pants (bistretch or wool-blend fabric; full length; classic slim boot or straight shape)

• Jeans (dark wash, skinny cut) **>>**

• Flat-front pants (no pleats!)

• White jeans

• Modest shorts (for weekends) **>**

SKIRTS AND DRESSES:

• Pencil skirt

• A-line skirt

• Miniskirt (see age guidelines in Chapter 2)

• Maxiskirt **>>**

• Wrap dress

• Little black dress

• Shift dress **>>**

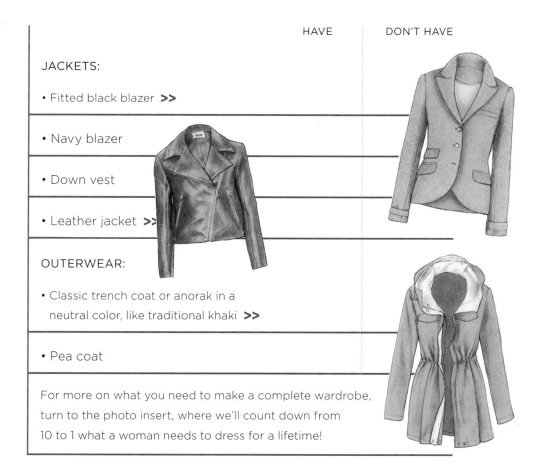

JACKETS:

• Fitted black blazer **>>**

• Navy blazer

• Down vest

• Leather jacket **>>**

OUTERWEAR:

• Classic trench coat or anorak in a
neutral color, like traditional khaki **>>**

• Pea coat

For more on what you need to make a complete wardrobe,
turn to the photo insert, where we'll count down from
10 to 1 what a woman needs to dress for a lifetime!

2. Alterable items that aren't perfect now but could be

So you've got a skirt that sits a little lower on the waist than you'd like.
Does a sizing issue like this mean you have to give the item to Goodwill?
No way! A simple alteration can give some clothes new life. Don't like the
cut of your pants anymore? Reinvent them! Do you have a bridesmaid
dress that would be wearable again in another color? Have it professionally
dyed. Zipper on your favorite bag break? A tailor or cobbler can likely fix
it for you.

Guide to What's Fixable (and What's Not)

Here are some common clothing problems and answers to whether or not a tailor can help you fix them.

Doable:

Anything that's too long. Hems are easy to take up, whether your sleeves go over your wrists, your pants drag on the floor, or your skirt hangs awkwardly below your knee. If you're taking up a pair of jeans, ask the tailor to reattach the original hem to avoid the DIY look.

Waist that gaps. If you've got a booty, chances are the waistline of your pants gapes open. Just have your seamstress cinch the waist.

Clothes that are too baggy. Often, the key to fixing a blouse that's *too* blousy or pants with more parachute than MC Hammer's is simply taking in the seams on the side. If necessary, your tailor can add darts to suck up additional fabric.

Garments missing buttons. If it's a simple style of button, your tailor may have a look-alike he or she can sew on. If not, head to your nearest fabric store and pick out new ones. Changing buttons is also an easy way to update a look!

Sometimes Doable:

Something that's too short. Sometimes, there's enough extra fabric to let out a hem by a smidge. But don't expect miracles: No tailor can give you an extra foot of length.

Voluminous jackets. If you mess too much with a certain style, you can lose the shape completely. Or the fix may require so much work in so many areas that it'll end up costing you a fortune.

Altering difficult-to-work-with fabrics. Another budget buster: thick or complicated fabrics like brocade, leather, or wool. Make sure the alteration is really worth the price before going through with it.

Reducing the size significantly. Found the perfect dress for your best friend's wedding—but it's six sizes too big? Or did you undergo a dramatic weight loss? While it's technically possible to make anything smaller, the downside is that you might lose some of the detailing that made you love the garment in the first place. Embellished edges might not be salvageable, or certain details or patterns might hit higher or lower on your body than was originally intended, so keep that in mind before you try.

Not Doable:

Clothes that are too small. The only way to make clothes bigger is to buy bigger clothes. Do yourself a favor and go up a size; then have the garment tailored to fit if it's a little too large. (Or if you shrunk the item in the wash, refer to the instructions on page 95 to try to resuscitate it.)

Camel toe. If the crotch of your pants is riding high and tight, there's nothing your tailor can do about it. Save both of you the embarrassment of even asking.

Shoes

A good cobbler can work wonders on your shoes. Did you know that, in addition to polishing and cleaning, a shoe-repair expert can perform the following fixes?

Replace the cap of your heel if you've worn it down to the nail

Add a heel shield (which can be dyed to match the shoe) to protect from scuffing and scratching

Replace the entire sole (or half sole)—a great option for expensive shoes you want to make last

Add rubber sole guards to make shoes slip resistant and more comfortable

Recondition leather or dye shoes to another color

Stretch the shoes if they're too tight in certain areas

Do other leatherwork, including shorten belts, repair luggage, stitch purses, and condition leather jackets

3. Clothes you love to wear that fit into your daily life

The most important thing here is to be realistic! Remember the honest talk we had with ourselves in the last chapter about age, geography, and lifestyle? Does the item you're hanging on to work with all three? If not, limit yourself to a handful of the x-factor items we discussed. A closet full of outliers won't do you any good in the long run.

Store

The fashion world is a cyclical one. Though no one would dare revert to wearing corsets on a daily basis, fashions from the past are constantly rearing their heads (ugly or not) in modern society. It's also seasonal—most of what you wear in the summertime is not usable come January. That's why it makes sense to put away what you're not wearing at the time so as not to overwhelm your closet.

What Should I Store?

- **ANYTHING OUT OF SEASON.** Don't waste space in your closet with wool sweaters and tall boots when it's 105 degrees outside! Pack up anything you can't wear in the current climate and store it elsewhere. (If you rent a storage unit, spring for an indoor, temperature-controlled space, as extreme temperatures can damage or discolor fabrics.)

- **ANYTHING OUT OF STYLE THAT YOU WANT TO KEEP.** Crossing your fingers for bell-bottoms to make a comeback? Good luck! But if you have the space available, you can hang on to your worthwhile vintage pieces. Keep this in mind, though: Some vintage items get more special with age and look great in any period. These are usually high-quality garments and garments from a bygone era, rather than a flash-in-the-pan trends. For example, vintage lace gloves or a 1940s-era handbag would look lovely worked in with your current wardrobe. A leisure suit would not. Be choosy about the pieces you keep. Opt to throw out cheaply made items and keep only those that would last long enough to be seen by your granddaughter. Besides, just because something comes back around, that doesn't mean you need to wear it.

- **SPECIAL-OCCASION PIECES.** The gown you wore to the black-tie fund-raiser last year probably doesn't deserve full-time residence in your closet, and neither does your fur stole. Instead, keep special-occasion pieces like these that get worn only once in a blue moon in a separate but easily accessible place. (You never know when you'll get invited to the opera at the last minute!)

- **JEWELRY.** There are two types of jewelry I suggest storing, and two very different reasons for doing so.

  1. **Costume jewelry.** Old costume jewelry from parents or grand-parents is great to keep; putting on a rhinestone necklace can be such an easy way to add personality to an outfit. Because these don't get worn daily, for the same reasons as special-occasion wear, I suggest getting them out of the way to make room for the accessories you wear most often.
  2. **Fine jewelry.** Pieces with precious gemstones or delicate metals shouldn't be stored in the same catchall where you keep your acrylic Forever 21 earrings. Not only are they bound to get misplaced or damaged that way, but in the event of a fire, flood, or break-in, it's smart to have your valuables stored in a fireproof, waterproof safe.

How Should I Store These Items?

- **COATS.** Mend loose buttons or torn linings. Empty pockets of debris or gloves, which can stretch out the fabric over a summer. Have coats dry-cleaned to prevent stains or dirt buildup from becoming permanent, and remove the plastic dry-cleaner bag. Hang the coats on sturdy, wide hangers that won't stretch or create bends in the fabric. If you have issues with moths, put cedar blocks (a moth deterrent) in the area you plan to store them, or purchase hangers made out of cedar. Stuff the shoulders with tissue to keep them from getting misshapen. Place each coat in a cloth garment bag to protect against dust and debris. Plastic bags can be used for nylon or synthetic ski jackets. (To cut down on the space that puffy down coats and vests can take up, consider vacuum-sealed space-saver bags. When it's time to wear them again, simply put them in a steamy bathroom or in the dryer with a few tennis balls to help fluff them back up.)

- **CLOTHES.** Launder or dry-clean any items going into storage; not only will you keep stains from setting, but you'll also

Dollars & Sense

I'm about to make you—and your pocketbook—happy: You don't have to go to the dry cleaner as often as you think you do. If you prefer not to hand wash, sweaters that don't touch your skin really need to be cleaned only once or twice a season. Coats should be cleaned only when stained or when getting ready to store for the warmer months. Invest in a steamer (travel-size versions are considerably cheaper than stand-up varieties) and steam shirts and pants between dry cleanings to get wrinkles out. Not only are dry cleaners expensive, but many treat your clothes with harsh chemicals—so don't overdo it!

keep moths at bay. Group items by material and fold or roll neatly. Do not hang delicate items such as sweaters, which can become stretched and misshapen. Place items in under-bed or stackable garment boxes made of breathable materials. Tuck cedar chips or a lavender sachet in each box to deter moths.

- **PURSES.** Clean out a purse's interior thoroughly, emptying all pockets, filing any receipts, throwing away trash like gum wrappers and used tissues, and vacuuming out dust and debris that has gathered. Next, clean the exterior. For leather, use a leather cleaner to moisturize and condition the material. For suede, either use a suede shoe cleaner or simply brush with a suede brush. For cotton or silk, carefully spot-treat any stains. Make sure the bag is completely dry before storing. You may drop an air freshener or sachet inside to prevent the buildup of musty scents. Unbuckle buckles and unhook attachable straps, placing them inside the purse to prevent lasting imprints; wrap metal pieces in tissue. Stuff the bag with a T-shirt or tissue to help it keep its shape. If your purse came with a cloth bag, place the purse inside before storing to protect it from getting scratched or collecting dust; if you don't have a cloth bag, a pillowcase works just fine. Do not store purses in plastic bags, however, as it prevents them from breathing. Stack bags horizontally in a canvas box or wicker basket to allow for air flow.

- **SHOES.** Clean your shoes with the proper cleaner. Make sure the interior and exterior are entirely dry before storing. Insert shoe trees or stuff tissue paper in the toes to help them maintain their shape. Pad metal buckles or clasps with tissue paper to prevent impressions from forming. Then wrap shoes in tissue or bubble wrap. If you have their original box, you can store them there, or if you have closet space elsewhere, a hanging shoe divider works well. Otherwise, buy low-profile under-bed storage solutions or stackable storage containers made of breathable canvas or cardboard. Label the outside of the box with what's inside, or better yet, take a photo of the shoes and adhere it to the front.

- **JEWELRY.** Before you store your jewelry for the long term, you'll want to clean each piece. Choose a case with multiple compartments that is lined in a soft fabric like velvet, which is easy on jewelry. Consider wrapping each piece in tissue paper to prevent scratching or, to make viewing easier, storing each piece in a small, anti-tarnish plastic bag. Keep the case in a cool, dry place.

MERCHANDISING YOUR CLOSET

Now that your unwanted pieces are gone and your unneeded pieces are temporarily relocated, all that's left in your closet are items that will aid in your quest to be your best self. That's an accomplishment in itself! Give yourself a pat on the back—or better yet, a stiff drink! The next step is to make it pleasing and even fun to step into your closet so that you actually *look forward* to picking out an outfit. Imagine that!

Let's attack the most basic principles first. Think about the way stores display their goods: in pristine condition; hung neatly; evenly spaced; not overly stuffed with hangers pointing in all directions. Keep these guidelines in mind when setting the groundwork for your dream closet:

- **BUY SEVERAL DOZEN OF THE SAME TYPE OF HANGER,** as many as it takes to accommodate all your clothes, so that everything looks orderly and uniform. You'll be amazed what a difference this makes. Professional organizer Amanda Kuzak prefers slim velvet hangers.

- **IRON OR STEAM EVERY PIECE AFTER WASHING OR WEARING AND BEFORE HANGING UP.** I have items in my closet that I haven't worn in months, simply because they're wrinkled and I don't have time to press them in the morning! I know it sounds horrifically lazy, but when minutes matter, guess where I'm going to cut back in the mornings?

- **DON'T SQUEEZE SO MANY HANGERS ONTO A ROD THAT YOU CAN'T SEE ALL THE CLOTHES EASILY.** When rods are that overstuffed, it becomes more tempting to leave clothes on the floor rather than to bother trying to hang them back up. Whether they're crinkled up against other items or balled up on the floor, your nicely ironed clothes will end up wrinkled all over again. If you have too many clothes to fit comfortably in the space you have, get rid of some or put some in drawers.

Style Cents

Not only is steaming quicker and easier than ironing, but it's much easier on your clothes, too, especially delicate fabrics. I use the Conair Compact Fabric Steamer, which is available at Target for around $50.

Now you've got everything hung neatly, but there's no logical order or practical solutions for items that don't hang. Here's where you've got to get creative about how to make the most of your allotted space.

I'm assuming you don't have a fifteen-square-foot closet packed with every bell and whistle the Container Store's Elfa system has to offer. (A girl can dream, though!) So the way you organize your space is going to depend largely on what kind of setup you have. If you have only a single rod in a cramped closet, I strongly suggest adding a second bar below or on another wall. Tension rods can work in a pinch, but they tend to

> THE EASIER YOUR SYSTEM IS FOR YOU TO USE,
> THE EASIER IT'LL BE FOR YOU TO KEEP
> YOUR CLOSET NEAT AND ORGANIZED.

buckle under a great deal of weight. Instead, consider a hanging rod (see "The Closet Essentials," on page 123), which hooks onto a high rod to double your hanging space. If you rent your apartment, ask your landlord about adding another rod that will screw into the wall.

The key is maximizing the room you've got by being economical with space and storing things in an efficient and orderly way. Find a way that makes sense for your life and stick with it—the easier your system is for you to use, the easier it'll be for you to keep your closet neat and organized.

Hanging Garments

There are several different ways that hanging clothes are most commonly organized:

1. Like color with like color and arranged in the order of the rainbow.
2. Grouped by type or occasion. Maybe you group all your shirts together and all your pants together, or perhaps you put work clothes in one area, going-out clothes in another, and casual wear in a third.
3. Things you wear most often in front, with less popular items in the back.

Or you could use some combination of the three. I arrange my clothes first by type of garment, and then by color, going from lightest to darkest. I further subdivide by assigning each type of garment a permanent home. Dresses, blazers, and pants live in my "big" closet. My wardrobe contains my tops, skirts, and shorts—which are hung—along with my jeans, sweaters, T-shirts, and intimates—which are folded in drawers, with the things I wear most on top. Nice shoes and handbags are kept in my smaller wardrobe. Obviously your setup will be different from mine, so find a way that works for you and your home.

Sweaters

Whatever you do, don't hang your sweaters like you would hang a shirt. Hangers can leave bumps in the shoulders or stretch out a neck before you know it. Instead of hanging, use one of these methods:

- **ROLL YOUR SWEATERS AND PLACE THEM IN DRAWERS.** Rolling is better than folding because you can easily see what you've got and remove what you want without messing up the others.

- **FOLD YOUR SWEATERS AND SET THEM ON SHELVES,** if you have them. If the shelf is particularly tall, maximize your space by purchasing stackable drawers or tiered shelf dividers. That way, when you want to grab one that's not on the top, you're not knocking over the entire pile. If you have no shelves in your closet and you have rod real estate to spare, consider buying canvas shelves that hang from the bar to create shelf space.

- **FOLD YOUR SWEATERS OVER A PANT HANGER** to protect them from hanger burn, if hanging is your only option. Multitiered pant hangers are a great option for saving additional space.

Shoes

Like any woman worth her salt, I've got a lot of shoes, and finding room for all of them in my closet can be a problem! For your own closet, try these options:

- **OVER-THE-DOOR HANGING ORGANIZERS** are great because they make the most of a space that is often unused. Each individual pocket holds a single heel or a pair of flats or sandals.

- **A SHOE RACK OR A LOW-PROFILE SHELVING UNIT** is a wonderful way to organize shoes, especially if it's short enough that it can fit in the oft-underutilized space on the floor beneath your hanging items, or on a high shelf. Put shoes that you wear most often in the most easy-to-reach places, with special-occasion shoes in less accessible areas.

- **SOMETIMES YOU DON'T NEED TO REINVENT THE WHEEL.** If you held on to the original shoebox that your shoes came in, you can simply store them in there, stacking boxes atop one another on a shelf. If you're not sure what each box contains, take a picture of the shoes and adhere it to the exterior. Or for easier visibility, clear plastic covered bins or drawers are a convenient option that is acceptable for storing the shoes that get used regularly. (For long-term storage, though, you're better off choosing a more breathable container. See page 109 for more on storing.)

- **TALL BOOTS CAN BE HUNG USING SKIRT HANGERS;** just be sure you pad the spots that get gripped—you don't want hanger marks on the delicate material.

- **BUY A SKINNY TIERED SHELVING SYSTEM,** which can often hold ten or more pairs, designed specifically for shoes.

Belts

I love a good belt as much as the next girl. Thick, skinny, leather, suede, animal skin—I've got 'em all. But if you can't easily see what you have, you won't think to pair that adorable purple patent leather number with that sheath dress. Fortunately, there are a few good options:

- **THE BEST OPTION, IF YOU HAVE WALL SPACE, IS TO HANG HOOKS** (or better yet, an organizer that has many hooks) on the wall. This is the most visible and easily accessible place to hang your belts.

- **IF WALL SPACE IS AT A PREMIUM (OR NONEXISTENT),** there are hanging organizers that make good options as well. Some arrange hooks vertically, some horizontally, others in a 360-degree structure. Choose the one that works best for you.

Scarves

Scarves can make the perfect addition to a nearly complete outfit, and in the colder months, they offer just the right amount of warmth. But how do you keep them organized?

- **HONEYCOMB-STYLE HANGING RINGS** make great options for thicker scarves. Each can be seen, removed, and replaced easily.

- **FOLD OR ROLL SCARVES AND PLACE THEM IN A BIN OR BASKET,** which keeps them organized and makes any closet look neat.

- **PARTICULARLY FOR SILK SCARVES OR HANDKER-CHIEFS,** a drawer organizer can be a fantastic choice, creating individual slots for each folded or rolled scarf and making viewing, grabbing, and going a breeze.

Purses

With apologies to diamonds, I think handbags are a girl's real best friend. But once you've accumulated a collection, it can be hard to tame. My two cents:

- **IF YOU HAVE PURSES YOU USE MOST OFTEN,** find an easily accessible shelf to sit them on. Though it's tempting to hang purses on a hook or coat rack, this can warp the handles. Be sure to use shelf dividers to help keep the purses upright.

- **FOR THE PURSES YOU USE LESS OFTEN,** divide by type (clutches together, handbags together, etc.) and arrange them, side by side, in bins, boxes, or drawers. Stuff the bags with tissue or old T-shirts for shape retention and put them in either the cloth bag they came in or a pillowcase to protect delicate fabric from scratches and prevent dust from accumulating.

Jewelry

Is bridling your baubles about to give you a breakdown? Are you constantly searching for a matching earring or untangling knotted-up necklaces? Learn how to tame your collection in no time (once you've properly stored your fine jewelry—see page 113):

- **NECKLACES ARE BEST HUNG TO AVOID TANGLES.** Screw decorative hooks into a wall or create a pretty pegboard from which to dangle your strands. A tree branch—painted if you prefer and anchored in a jar filled with sand, rocks, or marbles—also makes

Fashionista

20s

40s

60s

CLASSIC

Bombshell

20s

60s

40s

ALL-AMERICAN

20s

40s

60s

20s

40s

60s

Feminine

20s

40s

60s

The Countdown to Style

Must-haves for a Modern Wardrobe

9 ACCESSORIES

SHOES 7

TOPS
10

8 BOTTOMS

6 JACKETS

5 BAGS

3 COATS

4 JEANS

2 DRESSES

1 SPLURGE

What, Where, Wear

Don't stuff your suitcase with needless nonessentials! Here are the key elements to FOUR DIFFERENT WEEK-END WARDROBES. ▶▶

WINE TASTING

The Extras

MOUNTAIN MISCHIEF

The Extras

SAILING AWAY

The Extras

BEACH BUMMING

The Extras

a useful, eye-catching way to hang necklaces or hooked earrings. (Remember, you want your closet to be as appealing to walk into as your favorite store. Brightening things up with pretty displays can go a long way toward achieving that end.)

- **CLEAR PLASTIC DRAWER ORGANIZERS** with compartments of varying (or even better, adjustable) sizes are great for easily viewing everything at once as well as keeping earring pairs together. If you prefer a more decorative display, use pretty teacups or small decorative plates to contain your pieces.

Miscellaneous

Just remember the three *B*'s: bins, baskets, and boxes. Placed on a shelf, these are great catchalls for random odds and ends you don't know what to do with; simply throw your wares in and marvel at how neat your closet looks!

Dress (Your Closet) for Success

We're not the only ones who want to be dolled up—outfit your closet with practical and useful style tools:

A bulletin board where you can post pictures of outfits you like for inspiration and quick go-to guides when you're getting dressed.

A calendar. If you're really anal about repeating outfits, you can track when you wore what. A calendar can also help you remember upcoming events that you'll need a special outfit for as well as oft-forgotten holidays when stores typically have big blowout sales.

A mirror—full-length if you have the space, partial if you don't.

A step stool to help you reach high shelves safely.

A clock. It's easy to lose track of time when you're trying to decide what to wear. Bonus points if it has an outdoor temperature display so you know what the weather's like without having to set foot outside.

Maintenance is key to keeping your closet clutter-free. Vow to put things back in their proper places. Remove items that you no longer wear on a monthly basis. And if you find that a certain system isn't working for you, by all means, change it! This can and should be an ever-evolving process of what suits your lifestyle best.

The Closet Essentials

My top picks for a picturesque closet (and a peaceful mind):

Double Hang Closet Rod, available at the Container Store for $9.99

Huggable Hangers, available at the Container Store for $9.99 for a pack of ten

Chrome 4-Tier Swing-Arm Pant Hanger, available at the Container Store for $8.99

IKEA's Bumerang wooden hangers are also a great option at $3.99 for an eight-pack

Solid Shelf Dividers (vertical), available at the Container Store for $6.99 for two

White Grid Stacking Shelves (horizontal), available at the Container Store for $5.99 to $10.99

Algot storage system featuring wire and mesh baskets, available at IKEA, starting from $26.99

Natural 3-Tier Grippy Shoe Rack, available at the Container Store for $29.99

Crystal Clear Over-the-Door Vinyl Shoe Organizer, available at Bed Bath and Beyond for $14.99

10-Pocket Canvas Shoe Organizer, available at Target for $12.99

6-Compartment Canvas Hanging Sweater Bag, available at the Container Store for $19.99

Natural Cotton Garment Bags, available at the Container Store for $9.99 to $27.99

Long Underbed Box with Wheels, available at the Container Store for $22.99

Komplement multiuse hanger (great for scarves), available at IKEA for $7.99

Woven Strap Totes storage baskets, available at Bed Bath and Beyond for $12.99 to $19.99

Slotted Interlocking Drawer Organizers, available at the Container Store for $5.99

Stacking Jewelry Tray System, available at the Container Store for $7.99 to $17.99

Walnut Tie and Belt Rack, available at the Container Store for $19.99

A Numbers Game

- **70/30:** the balance of basics to trends you should have in your closet
- **70 percent:** the amount of clothes in your closet that should be appropriate for your workplace, whether that's a corner office or a first-grade classroom
- **2 to 3:** the number of pieces each article of clothing you own should be able to be worn with

Once you're done getting organized—and this can take a few days—stand back and admire your work (and help yourself to a second round of that stiff drink). This is a great time to notice common factors among your clothes or what holes remain in your wardrobe. Does your closet look like Superman's, with ten versions of the same outfit all in a row, or does it look like your space is shared by Dr. Jekyll and Mr. Hyde? Is your palette surprisingly void of color, or are you lacking muted tones to help neutralize an outfit? Are your clothes basically basic or totally trendy?

If you answered yes to any of these closet questions, your balance of cut, color, and style is in some way out of whack. It's time to plug those holes with some smart, strategic shopping!

BUILDING YOUR SHOPPING IQ

Chapter 4

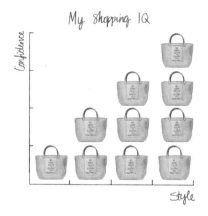

My Shopping IQ

Confidence

Style

I f you take shopping on a shoestring budget as seriously as I do, going to the mall can be a lot like playing in a championship sports match. You can't just show up the day of the big game and expect to be celebrating with champagne by the end of the night! To come out a winner, you need to have a rock-solid roster (in our case, a list of what you need—and *only* what you need), know your opponent's strategies (learn about retailers' tactics), understand the psychology of the sport (determine what makes us want to buy things), and, most of all, have a well-thought-out and executable game plan (decide in advance when, where, and how to shop).

So many of my friends and readers have said to me, "I wish you could go shopping with me so I'd know what to get!" As much as I'd love to accompany each and every one of you on your shopping excursions, I'd need a lot more free time (and a really forgiving husband)! So I'm going to do the next best thing: Beginning with this chapter and through the end of the book, I'm going to give you real, practical advice that you'll be able to put into practice when you shop, so it will feel like I'm actually there with you, holding your hangers and giving you pointers while you browse the racks. Whether you're a Sale-Only Chica, a Splurge Chica, a Sensible Chica, or a Spontaneous Chica, using my guiding principles, you'll be able to shop like the Cheap Chica!

Everything you've learned about budgeting, your body type, and your style up to this point, as well as all the prep work you've done (remember that big closet cleanout we did in the last chapter?), is going to help you become a better shopper. Using your freshly pruned closet and your personal fashion preferences, we'll determine your wardrobe needs and help you develop a shopping list that will act as a blueprint for your style. I'll also give you the tools you need to become an efficient and effective shopper—both in person and online—and teach you how to avoid common retail traps. All this before you even set foot in a store!

THE LIST

We use lists all the time: We make to-do lists to remind ourselves of what we need to accomplish, we scour best-dressed lists to see who's on the cutting edge of fashion, and, probably most common of all, we make grocery lists before we hit the supermarket. Much to my husband's dismay, I'm not much of a cook. Not even close. But on the rare occasions that I decide to use my kitchen for whipping up a meal rather

[IF WE SHOP FOR WHAT WE EAT THIS METICULOUSLY, WHY WOULDN'T WE SHOP FOR WHAT WE WEAR THE SAME WAY?]

than just storing my out-of-season sweaters, I wouldn't dream of going to the store without a list of what I need. I even bought myself one of those "All Out Of" notepads that has every kitchen item imaginable listed on it with a checkbox by each one, and I mark all the things I'm lacking so I don't get home and realize that I forgot a critical item that will keep me from completing my perfect meal.

My question is: If we shop for what we eat this meticulously, why wouldn't we shop for what we wear the same way? We've got so much on our minds these days that the last thing we have brain space for is memorizing the contents of our closets and which areas we need to plump up. Without a list, it's too easy to forget what you already have and what you still need—especially at the start of a new season, when all your clothes have been out of sight and mind for several months—which often leads to buying unnecessary items.

Behind the Scenes

Many of you have probably seen me do segments on *Today* and *The Rachael Ray Show*, but what you don't see is the amount of preparation that goes into each of those appearances. Whenever I have to style someone for TV, I make three lists before I even leave the house:

1. Before our initial interview I make a master list of items that I think would look good on my subject—including designer names and brands, as well as notes on fit.

2. Next we discuss what the subject feels most comfortable in and I prepare a combined list that blends his or her preferences with mine.

3. Lastly I come up with an alternative list for each item on the combined list, in case certain items aren't available. Having

alternatives is hugely important because it saves me from debating whether an item will work, helping me make quick and easy decisions on the spot. This becomes the final list that I take shopping with me.

Styling yourself will be easier, of course, since you know what you like and which cuts look best on you. But get into the habit of creating lists with this level of detail, which will take the guesswork out of shopping.

I find that the majority of my list making happens at the start of a new season, when I'm reevaluating what I own and thinking about what I'd like to add with the latest styles in mind. This is what a typical shopping list might look like for me each season, along with insights or advice about each entry:

Spring

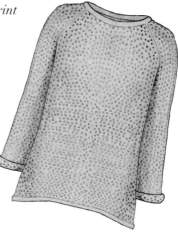

- **TRENCH COAT**

If you already have one in tan, pick one up in a fun print or bright color.

- **MAXISKIRT**

Great for any season, really. On chillier days, just add tights and boots.

- **OPEN-WEAVE SWEATER (IN CREAM)**

I love these layered over tanks, peeking out from under vests, and worn as swimsuit cover-ups in the summer.

- **NEW SUNGLASSES**

One of my favorite springtime purchases. While I don't spend a lot of money on them, a new pair can make me feel like a completely different woman!

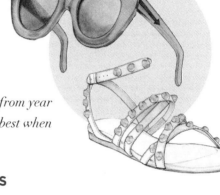

Summer

- **WHITE JEANS**

I've tried to carry them over from year to year, but they simply look best when they're crisp and new.

- **NUDE FLAT SANDALS**

I wear them with everything, so I can never have enough pairs.

- **BIKINI SEPARATES**

I try to buy two-pieces that I can wear together or mix and match with separates from the previous summer.

- **GOLD HOOP EARRINGS**

My go-to accessory on and off the beach. I always go cheap on these and buy them in three-pair sets (hello, Claire's boutique!).

Fall

- **TWEED BLAZER**

Even at thirty-three, I still don't quite feel like a grown-up. Mature blazers add major sophistication to my wardrobe.

- **BOOTS IN BROWN OR BLACK**

My preferred style is an ankle or knee boot—flat or with a moderate heel for maximum wearability.

- **PRINTED SCARF**

When you buy them for under $20 like I do, it's OK to have a closetful in different colors and prints! I love using them to update basic outfits like jeans and a T-shirt.

- **TIGHTS**

I wear through mine quickly, so I replace them every year. I start the season wearing black and dark gray and then move into patterns as the months progress.

Winter

- **STATEMENT NECKLACE**

My style is very relaxed in the winter (lots of leggings and sweaters), so it's nice to have something like a bold piece of jewelry to instantly transform my look from casual to chic.

- **CASHMERE SWEATER**

A new cashmere sweater is my once-a-year treat. I don't mind splurging a little, since it will last for years. Depending on my mood, I either go totally neutral or totally bright!

- **SOMETHING METALLIC**

While most people go for sequins at this time of year, I prefer a more subtle sparkle in the winter.

Now that you've seen how I prepare my lists, you're ready to start one of your own! The process will differ from person to person, as you determine what methods work best for you, but here are some key strategies:

1. Actually do it.

This list isn't going to magically materialize out of thin air—you have to take the initiative to start writing things down and then update it regularly. As you dress yourself each day, take note of the items you need in order to create exciting, inspiring outfits. Is that skirt missing a skinny yellow belt to punch it up? Is that cardigan not cutting it anymore? Make a note as soon as you notice a lapse in your wardrobe. When you do seasonal closet cleanouts, write down things that are past their prime or that you've outgrown.

2. Be specific.

Don't say that you need "shirts for work." That could mean a zillion different things. Instead, note that you need a black silk blouse or a blue cashmere V neck. The more specific you can be, the harder it will be to excuse an extraneous purchase. But remember to give yourself options so that if the exact item you dreamed up doesn't exist in stores, you can find something similar that will work.

3. Fill in the gaps.

Is your wardrobe looking rather blue, or does it leave you seeing red? Does the shape of your skirts read like the report card of a straight-A student, or does it more closely resemble a box of No. 2 pencils? Find the common color, cut, and style threads in your closet and make an effort to buy what you don't have in adaptations that will look best on you.

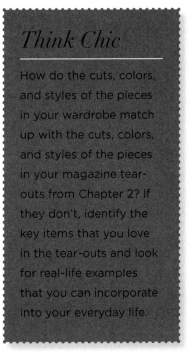

Think Chic

How do the cuts, colors, and styles of the pieces in your wardrobe match up with the cuts, colors, and styles of the pieces in your magazine tear-outs from Chapter 2? If they don't, identify the key items that you love in the tear-outs and look for real-life examples that you can incorporate into your everyday life.

> [FIND THE COMMON COLOR, CUT, AND STYLE
> THREADS IN YOUR CLOSET AND MAKE AN
> EFFORT TO BUY WHAT YOU DON'T HAVE IN
> ADAPTATIONS THAT WILL LOOK BEST ON YOU.]

4. Balance.

Remember to maintain the 70/30 basics-to-trends ratio (though there are exceptions to this ratio; see Chapter 5 for more). If you've got your staples covered, it's OK to mix in some bolder choices, but if you're overrun with trendy items, your list should be heavy on neutral, long-lasting options. (For a full list of basics every woman should have, refer to Chapter 3.)

5. Plan ahead.
Check the calendar for upcoming events you'll need a special outfit for—weddings, parties, holidays, and the like. Even if they're months down the line, begin looking for appropriate items now to avoid breaking the bank when you're desperate later.

Once you've gotten in a list-making groove, step up your game with some advanced, outside-the-box dressing. Your wardrobe and your resulting shopping list will reflect a certain side of your style—but don't be afraid to push yourself. Experimenting with different looks will keep you from falling into a style rut.

For instance, if you gravitate toward a bohemian style of dress, your list of staples might be different from that of someone who identifies herself as a classic dresser. But a little genre bending can be a great thing! Try incorporating some rock-star notes into your wardrobe or a preppy piece here and there for a fashionable and contemporary twist.

If you need some inspiration, I've created two shopping lists for each of the six styles we outlined in Chapter 2. (Don't remember what you are? Retake the quiz on page 52) The first is what a typical list might look like for you, and the second is a list of things to consider incorporating into your wardrobe.

RISK TAKER:
Totally Trendy—and a Slave to Style

What's probably on your list:

1. Motorcycle jacket
2. Lots of black
3. Structured separates
4. Sky-high stilettos
5. Leather pants

What should be on your list:

1. **FLATS**
Give those heels a rest and mix in a pair of flats with edgy details like studs or embellishment.

2. SOFT SKIRTS (CHIFFON OR SILK)
These will contrast nicely with some of your tougher pieces!

3. PALE-PINK CARDIGAN
Who says high-end fashion can't be girly?

4. SILK BOYFRIEND BLOUSE
Unlike many of your trendier tops, a classic piece like this will stand the test of time.

5. WHIMSICAL PRINTS
Hearts, polka dots, and anchors will help make your look more playful.

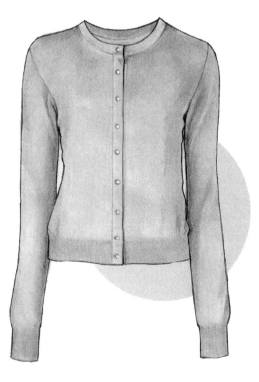

MINIMALIST:
A Timeless Beauty in Need of Some Modern Updates

What's probably on your list:

1. Straight-leg jeans
2. Button-down shirts
3. Neutral colors
4. Practical shoes
5. Totes

What should be on your list:

1. **SEQUIN SKIRT**
Your clothes deserve to have fun sometimes! Pair this with a classic-cut top, which you've got loads of, and you'll look flirty (and not *like a floozy).*

2. **ANYTHING IN COBALT BLUE**
This shade is a new neutral—it goes with everything and can be worn year-round.

3. **ANKLE BOOTIES**
This is an easy and fairly risk-free way to liven up your footwear.

4. BANDAGE SKIRT
Show off that figure! This is sure to add a little va-va-voom to your look.

5. A RED DRESS
This eye-catching number has been a favorite for decades.

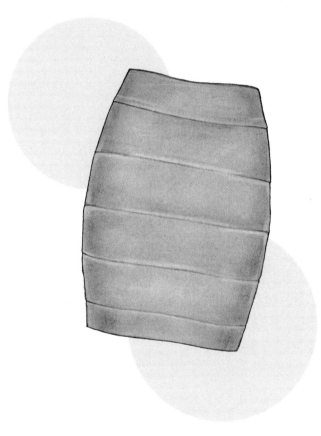

SHOWSTOPPER:
Always Sassy but Could Stand to Get Classy

What's probably on your list:

1. Figure-hugging dresses
2. Skinny jeans
3. Animal prints
4. Platform shoes
5. Bandage skirts

What should be on your list:

1. A MAXISKIRT
Sometimes less skin is sexiest.

2. OVER-THE-KNEE FLAT BOOTS
This choice is still hot but much more practical than the sky-high stilettos you're used to.

3. BOYFRIEND SWEATER
Baggy does not have to equal boring. Use this to tone down a sexier skirt.

4. TROUSERS
Your work clothes shouldn't call out for attention. Classic-cut trousers indicate that you're professional without sacrificing style.

5. POLKA DOTS

Nothing says "sweet" like this timeless pattern, so incorporate a little into your edgier outfits for balance.

GIRL NEXT DOOR:
The Collegiate Look That's Ready to Graduate

What's probably on your list:

1. Striped anything
2. Boat shoes
3. Shift dresses
4. Cardigans
5. Blazers

What should be on your list:

1. LEATHER OR PLEATHER PANTS
Get wild, child! In a figure-hugging (but not body-squeezing) cut, these can instantly edge up a look without crossing over into skanky territory.

2. LACE
Adding texture to your basics will take them to the next level.

3. PRINTED JEANS
You're familiar with denim—now meet their fun-loving cousin.

4. ANIMAL-PRINT ACCESSORIES

Dare to pair prints. If you're wearing plaid, mix it with a dotted leopard print. Rocking a floral dress? Incorporate zebra stripes!

5. METALLICS

Nothing pumps up a preppy look like adding a silver shoe or a gold clutch.

ROMANTIC:
Epitomizes Ladylike but Lacks an Edge

What's probably on your list:

1. A-line or full skirts
2. Lace blouses
3. Pretty pumps
4. Trench coats
5. Peplums

What should be on your list:

1. LACE-UP OXFORDS
There's nothing hotter than a woman who can pull off menswear, and shoes are a great place to start.

2. TUXEDO BLAZER
Look like a VIP with a crisp, tailored version of this classic masculine cut.

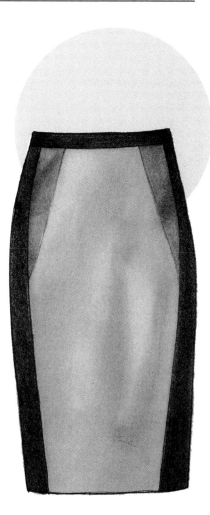

3. LEATHER JACKET

This choice provides the perfect way to roughen up around the edges.

4. PENCIL SKIRT

Try this sexier silhouette for the gal who usually tends toward girly.

5. NEON BELT

Your closet of soft shades could use a bold punch.

HIPPIE CHIC:
Flower Power That's Ready to Bloom

What's probably on your list:

1. Maxiskirts/dresses
2. Silk blouses
3. Flat sandals
4. Boot-cut jeans
5. Hobo bags

What should be on your list:

1. NAVY BLAZER
Add some structure to your life with a well-cut jacket. Paired with your loose-fitting separates, it makes for an effortlessly chic look.

2. LACE BUSTIER
The polar opposite of soft and flowy, this top is guaranteed to wow.

3. NUDE PUMPS
These are a dummy-proof way to dress up your look for dates, interviews, or cocktails.

4. SKINNY JEANS
Form-fitting denim is your friend.

5. PRINTED TROUSERS
Skirts are great, but tailored trousers lend an air of power and professionalism.

Just a few additions to your closet like the items listed here can go a long way. To see the proof, turn to the photo insert to see The Lucky 13: how I transform thirteen pieces into a month's worth of looks!

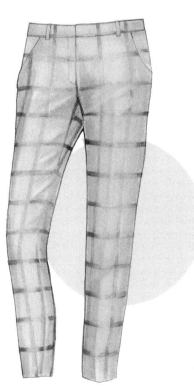

MONEY MATTERS

Now that you know what you need, your next step is as simple as going shopping, buying just those items, and heading home a happy customer, right? If only! Unfortunately for us, merchandisers are master manipulators when it comes to breaking down our resolve and convincing us to buy more than we intended to. While you can't change the way stores operate, you can make yourself aware of the methods at work so you're able to resist the temptations they present—or use them to your advantage.

First, a quick primer in Retail 101. The obvious goal of any commercial operation is to make money. That's true whether you're talking about a corporate behemoth like Exxon-Mobil or your neighborhood yogurt shop. The way retail enterprises make a profit is to buy clothes at a low

> MERCHANDISERS ARE MASTER MANIPULATORS WHEN IT COMES TO CONVINCING US TO BUY MORE THAN WE INTENDED TO.

cost from manufacturers and then mark up the sales price—sometimes by as much as 70 or 80 percent—so that they make a pretty penny in the end. So let's say a pair of jeans costs $15 to manufacture. The retailer might purchase them from the manufacturer for $20 apiece and then sell them to you for $90. That means that they make a profit of $70 per pair! Retailers are always striving for a high **gross margin percentage,** which is profit expressed in a percentage. In the example just given, the gross margin percentage would be 78 percent. Said another way, the store got to keep $0.78, or more than three-fourths, of every dollar it spent. (How did I come to this number? See the sidebar for an explanation.)

But it doesn't stop there. The men and women running these stores know that seeing a pair of $90 jeans hanging on a rack isn't going to make you whip out your wallet. So they employ a number of psychological tactics to fool you into thinking you're getting a better deal than you actually are. They play on our desire to feel like we're getting a bargain. What types of tricky maneuvers should you be on the lookout for? Here are a few of the most common:

Fake Sales

The tactic: If a store wants to sell a dress for $60, they might put a price of $85 on the tag and immediately mark the item on "sale" for the intended asking price of $60. This is especially common in outlets and on flash-sale websites (see Chapter 6 for more on both). Why go through the extra trouble? Because even if something isn't particularly cheap, they know that if we think we're getting a deal, we're all too happy to jump on it!

How to outsmart it: Don't be automatically swayed by so-called discount prices. Research the price points of your desired items ahead of time so you know what you should expect to pay. Consider a purchase only if its current price is reasonable and within your budget. If it's a brand that's carried by multiple stores, comparison shop to see which retailer has the better price.

More for Less

The tactic: Say you walk into Victoria's Secret looking for two new pairs of panties. They're priced at $7 apiece, so you grab two pairs and start heading for the register when you notice a sign that says FIVE FOR $25. You quickly do the math and

Style Cents

"Come back soon" isn't just a familiar phrase on store signage—it's also good advice for smart shopping. The more you shop your favorite stores, the more familiar you'll become with their practices. Were you just there last week, and merchandise you're seeing for the first time is already on sale? You'll know it may not be the steal that new customers think it is.

realize that, for $11 more, you could go home with an extra three pairs, prompting you to dig through the piles for three more thongs that you don't really need. Stores often do this to encourage you to buy more than you ordinarily would have, and their high markups prevent them from losing any money on the transaction.

How to outsmart it: It's easier to resist falling into this trap when you're armed with your shopping list. Though deals like these can be worthwhile if the product really is something you need to stock up on, if you're having to *find* things to buy, it's not worth the savings.

BOGOs

The tactic: The well-known "buy one, get one" deals have been a staple of salesmanship for years. Whatever iteration they come in—buy two, get one free; buy one, get one 50 percent off; buy two, get a free bonus gift—the idea is the same: send you home with more than you need. As with the "more for less" strategy, if you really need two pairs of boots and you find two pairs you love, this tactic can prove fruitful for you. But if you were satisfied with your single pair and get talked into a second just to get a third for free, you're going to end up with a bunch of boots you don't really like taking up precious space in your once-tidy closet.

How to outsmart it: Refer to your trusty shopping list when temptation becomes overwhelming. Being reminded of what other items you're looking to score will encourage you not to blow your entire budget in one department.

Spend More to Save More

The tactic: You've likely seen it time and time again in many a retail store: save $25 on any purchase over $100, $50 on any purchase over $150, or $75 on any purchase over $200. These tiered approaches can be very effective, making you feel justified in taking everything from the dressing room home with you rather than weeding it down to the best of the best. The fact of the matter is, even if you're saving a few extra bucks the higher your bill climbs, you're still spending more in the end.

WHEN THE SALES ASSOCIATE DOES HER BEST TO UP-SELL YOU, SMILE POLITELY AND RECITE THESE TWO SIMPLE WORDS: "NO, THANKS."

How to outsmart it: Forget the savings amounts and decide what items you'd buy even at full price. Take those items to the register, no matter what price tier you're in—or how close you are to the next. And when the sales associate does her best to up-sell you, smile politely and recite these two simple words: "No, thanks."

Haute Hint

Some boutiques will display magazine tear-outs of a celebrity wearing one of their items or a garment from their collection featured in a fashion spread. This isn't just for bragging rights: They know that seeing style authorities hawk the very item we're holding in our hands will trigger our "gotta have it" response. Take the same approach we do for all our savvy shopping:

Ask yourself:

1. Do I love this?
2. Would I buy it even if Jessica Alba didn't wear it on the red carpet?
3. Does it fit and flatter *my* body?
4. Is it in my budget?
5. Can I wear it with at least three items already in my closet?

If you answered yes to all five questions, it's still a good buy.

SALES VERSUS MARKDOWNS

Y ou're probably well versed in what a sale is. We get bombarded with announcements of them all the time in TV commercials, in the newspaper, in our e-mail in-boxes, and on store signage: limited-time-only price reductions that will revert back to original levels once the discount period is over. These "act now" incentives trigger rash and irresponsible decision making in the best of us—it's human nature!

A markdown, on the other hand, is a different type of discount altogether. This price reduction is usually reserved for a piece that isn't selling well—either because it's an unpopular style or because there's some defect in the garment—or for leftover items at the end of a season that must be sold to make way for new goodies. The goal of retail stores is to be out of merchandise with every changing season, so when a product isn't moving as fast as they'd like, they put it on deep discount in an effort to rid themselves of the remainders.

This isn't to say you should ignore markdowns; sometimes these clearance prices can be a blessing for your budget. In particular, markdowns are great ways to save on expensive designer items and trendy or out-of-season pieces with a short shelf life. With markdowns, as with any other discount

Haute Hint

Most department stores have major sales events only two to three times a year. Nordstrom, for instance, has half-yearly sales for men, women, and children and an anniversary sale in July. Saks and Bloomingdale's have "friends and family" sales, typically two or three times annually, that are open to the public. But Macy's takes the trophy when it comes to sales, hosting numerous one-day events throughout the year.

purchase, be smart about what you buy. Try everything on to make sure it fits well, and inspect each item for imperfections (we'll talk more about what to look for in Chapter 5). If you shop online, obviously these tips are impossible, so make sure you check the store's return policy. If the items are final sale (online or in person), you'll want to be doubly sure that this is a piece that will complement your wardrobe and get lots of wear.

YOUR SHOPPING SCHEDULE

The next step in your shopping strategy is to figure out *when* to spend. I'm not talking about just time of day (though going to the mall during the workday or on a weeknight is always going to yield better results than trying to fight the weekend crowds). I'm talking about breaking down your shopping schedule month by month and even day by day to get the best deals. That's right—the day you buy something can determine how much money you save on it. So clear your calendars and get ready to start saving!

Daily

In addition to your LOLs and OMGs and TTYLs, I've got one more acronym I want you to remember: TGIT. No, that's not a typo. With all due respect to Friday, I say, thank goodness it's Thursday, and so should you. That's when most stores restock their supplies and begin to mark things down for weekend sales, making Thursday the optimum day to hit the shops.

Online retailers don't have the same weekend shopping surges as brick-and-mortar stores, and therefore they don't have the same sale schedules either. Less predictability can make for more confusing bargain shopping. But fear not! One of my favorite online fashion resources, an amazing site called ShopItToMe.com (whose praises I'll sing more in the next section), conducted a survey to see when the best deals are to be had online. Here's what they found:

ITEM	BEST DAY FOR DEALS	AVERAGE DISCOUNT
Women's dress pants	Monday	48 percent
Sunglasses	Monday	55 percent
Men's apparel	Tuesday	42 percent
Shoes	Wednesday	38 percent
Kids' clothing	Wednesday	40 percent
Handbags	Thursday	36 percent
Accessories	Friday	42 percent
Intimates	Saturday	37 percent
Outerwear	Saturday	51 percent
Swimwear	Sunday	52 percent

Monthly

Almost like clockwork, around the same time every year, retailers discount certain seasonal items or start rolling out new inventory. Knowing when this happens is crucial to any shopping strategy. Here's a breakdown:

DECEMBER/JANUARY

At the turn of each year, stores begin to liquidate their winter gear—coats, gloves, scarves, hats, and boots. You may have to hunt to find your size, but there are good deals to be had if you're willing to look. The prices drop the longer you wait, but naturally, so does the selection. Following the post-holiday rush is also a great time to buy cocktail dresses.

Potential savings: 50 to 70 percent

FEBRUARY

In addition to offering good deals on jewelry and lingerie (hey, at least Valentine's Day is good for something!), retailers begin to roll out their spring styles this month. Start window-shopping the new trends so you know what's going to be hot, and then start looking for items you're interested in at lower prices. The best part about this kind of preview shopping? It's free! If you see some lingering winter items that could transition to spring, snag them now while they're at their cheapest.

Potential savings: 30 to 40 percent

Style Cents

If you're shopping at a national chain and your local retailer doesn't have your size, ask a salesperson to do a systemwide search for your item. Often, the store rep can find it at another location and have it shipped to you. (Most will provide free shipping, as well.)

MARCH/APRIL

Spring fever can sway even the most steadfast saver, but resist the urge to slap down your credit card for a whole new wardrobe. Instead, write down two to three key items (like I did earlier in my seasonal shopping list example) and what you're willing to spend on them. Early in any season you can count on the best selection in styles and sizes, so if you see something you love and it's within your budget, you're allowed a few full-price splurges to build the rest of your wardrobe around.

This is also a great time to buy early-markdown spring shoes, as well as sneakers, thanks to the rush of irregular exercisers (like me) who are starting to panic about the impending beach season.

Potential savings: 20 to 30 percent

MAY

It's spring-cleaning season, making it the perfect time to hit up your local thrift shops and consignment stores. An influx of donations means a better selection—and better prices—for you. Vintage gems like furs, jewelry, and handbags are great for snatching up this month.

Potential savings: 50 to 70 percent

JUNE/JULY

Summer sales are in full swing, so scour the racks for anything you can still get good wear out of—shorts, sundresses, a flirty romper, or those sandals you've been lusting after will be heavily discounted. The first fall items will be starting to hit the racks, so begin browsing for inspiration and think about what items you have in storage that you'll want to keep around for another year.

Potential savings: 25 to 40 percent

Style Cents

When you find something you love at a great price—that pair of jeans that makes your booty beautiful, those shoes that you wear with everything—don't be afraid to buy two pairs! Classic styles that recur year after year are worth stocking up on!

With others, once they're out of the store, they're gone forever. Consult a sales associate you trust to see if he or she knows if a cut or style of a particular item you love is returning. If not, better to buy a backup now than risk ruining your only one later.

AUGUST/SEPTEMBER

Stores are eager to clear out summer leftovers to make room for back-to-school items and other fall staples, so pick up white jeans, shorts, tanks, and swimsuits on major discount for next year. Sizes are limited by this point, so be ready to dig. You can also find some initial promotions (15 percent) on new fall items, but hold out if you can.

Potential savings: 40 to 60 percent

OCTOBER

With the rush for back-to-school shopping over, retailers begin cutting prices on remaining inventory, which includes a lot of basics that you can wear year-round. This is the best time to score jeans at a discount. Smaller holidays like Columbus Day often mean sales too.

Potential savings: 40 to 60 percent

NOVEMBER

Save your shopping energy for the mother of all sale events: Black Friday and Cyber Monday. Take the opportunity to stock up on luxe and lust-worthy essentials like cashmere while you can actually afford them! Your wallet will thank you, even if it means braving the mall with the masses.

Potential savings: 30 to 40 percent

DECEMBER

The holidays and end-of-year earnings reports mean that retailers are in major markdown mode. Take advantage of these sales not just for people on your gift list but for yourself as well.

Potential savings: 30 to 50 percent

Haute Hint

Shopping on Black Friday isn't for the faint of heart. Here are a few tips for those of you fearless enough to brave the post-Thanksgiving rush:

- In addition to what's listed in the Black Friday ads that circulate in newspapers, many stores list extra "secret" deals on their websites Thanksgiving Day.
- Bring a friend with you and team up. Have your friend wait in the inevitably long line while you shop; then switch.
- Don't forget that you can likely get similar deals just three days later on Cyber Monday from the comfort of your home or office. There's no reason to risk life and limb for a good deal.

GAME PLAN:
IN THE STORE

The last step before you've earned the right to go shopping is to develop a plan for how you're going to tackle each store. To cut out some of the confusion, I like to start out at department stores. They've got everything under one roof, which makes building an outfit easy and, best of all, quick. When I'm in a rush, I can efficiently hop from department to department, seeing how pieces look together and which shoes and accessories work best with an outfit, then check out one time rather than at every stop along the way. Department stores also generally have better sales than smaller boutiques because they have the most inventory to move.

If I can't find what I'm looking for in a department store, I'll then work my way through nearby stores or hit up various boutiques around town. What I'm shopping for determines how leisurely a pace I adopt and how many stores I hit. If I've got a very targeted search, I'll stick to stores that I know carry the styles I'm looking for so as not to waste time— or tempt myself—by venturing into stores I'm less familiar with. If I'm scouting for seasonal trends, however, I'll allow myself to explore a little more, checking out places I've never been to in hopes that I'll discover a new resource for future needs. Then I'll hit up my girl-on-a-budget go-tos, like Target, T.J.Maxx, Nordstrom Rack, and consignment shops (for a full list of stores that carry the best steals, turn to Chapter 6).

No matter where I go, though, my plan is usually the same. Depending on what's on your list, tailor my methods to fit your needs:

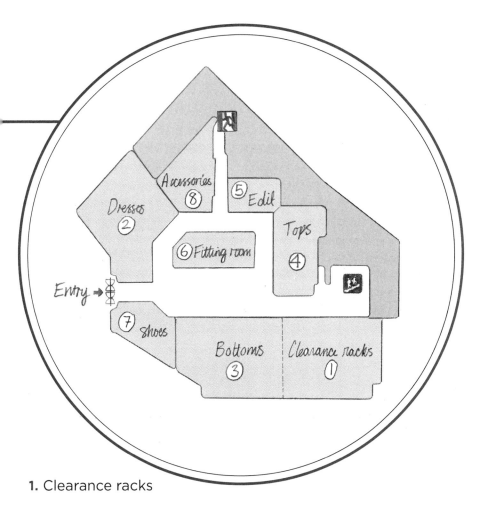

- Accessories (8)
- Dresses (2)
- Edit (5)
- Tops (4)
- Fitting room (6)
- Entry →
- Shoes (7)
- Bottoms (3)
- Clearance racks (1)

1. Clearance racks

If you learn just one thing from me in this whole book, let it be this: Shop the clearance racks first. Do not allow yourself to get distracted by all the pretty, shiny new things in front. Instead, go straight to the sale racks in the back—no excuses. When you start in the discount section, you will set your "price barometer" as high as possible. After seeing prices that are discounted 50 to 70 percent, you'll find that a full-priced item seems like a huge rip-off (as it probably is).

2. Dresses

Once I've exhausted all the markdown items, I go in search of dresses. Why? Because they're an all-in-one outfit! Even if you're not skilled at mixing pieces, shopping for dresses will boost your mood and confidence, and you'll be off to a great start.

3. Bottoms

Next I hunt for bottoms: trousers, jeans, skirts, and shorts. The wide variety of cuts, lengths, details, colors, and prints means you'll need a lot of patience, which you'll have near the start of your search.

4. Tops

The last items I grab before I try on are tops. I follow the KISS (keep it simple, stupid) approach and gravitate toward shirts that can go with at least five things in my closet, which makes getting dressed easier and your bill smaller!

5. Edit

Now you've got to decide which pieces you pulled actually get the privilege of seeing you (almost) naked! I'm a firm believer that you shouldn't edit at the rack. Instead, grab whatever items appeal to you based on your initial instincts and pare down your picks right before you head into the dressing room.

6. Fitting room

As I told the Sale-Only Chicas in Chapter 1, you should be wearing clothes that are easy to get into and out of, as well as appropriate undergarments for whatever you're trying on. In most cases, a thong is going to be your best bet to avoid panty lines or bunching. Once you've got your potential purchases on, check yourself out from all angles. Walk, bend, sit, stretch, squat—do whatever you'll need to be able to do in your clothes if you take them home with you. Pay close attention to the fit—is it pulling or cutting you off anywhere? Is the button placket open? Are the sleeves too short or the shoulders too far in? Inspect the items for any defects, such as stains or snags. Don't like the light in your dressing room? Step outside and find a place where you can see yourself clearly.

And as tedious as it may seem, try everything on. Even if an item is the trendiest thing going and it's a great price, if it doesn't look good on you, you shouldn't buy it. Period!

7. Shoes

While this is easily my favorite section of any store, you have no business starting here on a typical shopping trip. The only time that's an acceptable practice is when you're specifically shopping for new shoes. Otherwise, remember: A new pair of shoes does not an outfit make! If you allow yourself to splurge on shoes first, you might end up blowing your entire budget.

8. Accessories

This is the time to "successorize" your purchases with items like jewelry, belts, and scarves. But remember to save here rather than splurge: Most accessories are trendy and will change from season to season. (Plus, your best friend probably has something you can borrow that would work just as well.)

In addition to knowing what order to attack the store in, the smartest shoppers have some secrets that you can employ when you go bargain hunting, as well. Remember these pointers when you venture out:

- **LOOK GOOD!** As I said earlier, you're never going to love what you're trying on if your hair is wet and you're self-conscious about your outfit. Make an effort before you go to the mall—a little lip gloss, a nude thong, and a hairbrush go a long way! The more you like the way you look in your old clothes, the more likely you are to like the way you look in your soon-to-be-new clothes.

- **AIM TO LIMIT YOUR TRIPS TO TWO HOURS OR LESS.** After that point, your resolve drops, and you'll end up buying something just to make the trip feel worthwhile.

- **IF YOU MUST BE OUT LONGER, PACK A SNACK.** Hunger leads to grumpiness, so give your brain the boost it needs when your stamina gets low.

- **FOCUS ON ONE GOAL AT A TIME.** Rather than shopping for work clothes, casual wear, and going-out gear all in the same trip (which can muddle your mission), shop for only one type of clothing per outing. That way, when you scan a store, you'll know exactly which items to look at more closely and which to ignore (until your next visit, that is).

- **COME PREPARED.** Wear or bring the right accessories, undergarments, and shoes for whatever you're trying on. If you're attempting to match a shirt to a skirt, bring the top with you so you're not guessing if the skirt you've got in your sights looks good with the top you have in your closet. If you're trying on gowns, bring a strapless bra—but not your sneakers.

- **YOU'RE NOT FORBIDDEN FROM ENTERING THE HIGH-PRICED STORES;** just keep your wallet under wraps. Instead, get inspiration from the designer brands and then find the same look for less at another, less expensive retailer.

- **ALWAYS, ALWAYS, ALWAYS FIND OUT A STORE'S RE-TURN POLICY.** If it's nonexistent, be extra careful about what you buy. File your receipts when you get home in a way that works for you.

- **USE COUPONS!** If the store's not having a sale, make your own by strategically using promotional coupons you get in the mail, in the store, and off the Web. Some stores, like Lord & Taylor, will even text a coupon code to your phone. And don't be shy—ask the salesperson if there are any coupons you can use!

Savings on Top of Savings

Are you an aspiring couponing queen? Here are some tips on how to make the most of your discounts:

Expand your search beyond the Sunday paper. Don't throw away the flyers salespeople stick in your shopping bags along with your receipts—many times they're loaded with coupons!

Check the website before you buy. There might be an online-only sale going on, and sometimes retailers have printable coupons on their sites that you can use in-store.

When making a purchase online, check sites like Poachit.com or RetailMeNot.com for discount codes.

Be strategic. If a store accepts multiple coupons for the same transaction, be sure to present them in the most advantageous order. Hand over a percentage-based coupon before a dollar-amount discount—the bigger the total, the more money you'll save with a percentage-based coupon. And pay attention to minimum purchase amounts dictated by your coupons; if you're required to spend $100 to get the deal, don't give the salesperson other coupons first that will reduce your total.

Say yes to retail e-mail. Make sure you're on your favorite stores' mailing lists so you can be up-to-date on the latest sales. To avoid an overflowing in-box, create a dedicated e-mail address for these blasts or have them route straight into a folder you've created specifically for these types of e-mails.

Take advantage of price adjustments. If a price is reduced within fourteen days of your purchase, most stores will refund you the difference if you present a receipt.

Be prepared. If a sales associate is giving you trouble, having the store's coupon policies printed out will help your case. Don't hesitate to ask for a manager if need be.

Style Cents

When you find salespeople you love, make friends! Find out their work schedules and always ask for them when you visit their stores. They can give you a heads-up about upcoming sales, hold items for you, and notify you when styles you'd like or sizes you need come in.

GAME PLAN: ONLINE

For many of you technophiles, the idea of actually setting foot in a store might seem like an archaic practice that amounts to a giant waste of time. You're probably asking, "Why would I shop at one place at a time when I can shop the entire world from the comfort of my couch?"

True, online shopping offers a wider range of brands, styles, and prices than any store ever could. With the click of a mouse and the right websites, you could buy a new wardrobe without ever getting out of your pajamas. Of

> [WITH THE CLICK OF A MOUSE AND THE RIGHT WEBSITES, YOU COULD BUY A NEW WARDROBE WITHOUT EVER GETTING OUT OF YOUR PAJAMAS.]

course, old-school shoppers will argue that the ability to try pieces on, getting to feel the fabrics, and the ease of returns make the in-person experience worth any inconvenience. But if you prefer surfing the World Wide Web to walking the mall, here are the best ways to navigate your virtual shopping trip:

1. **FOR ME, EVERY ONLINE PURCHASE STARTS AT SHOPSTYLE .COM,** an aggregator of web retailers. Simply type in what you're looking for—whether it's as specific a search as *white Marc Jacobs hobo bag* or as general as *patent pumps*—and the site pulls up thousands of options from around the web. Once it's returned your results, you can filter them by color, price, markdown, and size. If you're not ready to buy, simply bookmark an item to your "Looks" folder for easy access later.

2. **ONCE I'VE NARROWED MY SELECTION** to the perfect piece, it's off to RetailMeNot.com to perform a quick coupon-code search. With so many resources out there to help you cut costs, you should expect to shave off at least the shipping fee from each purchase!

3. **IF I ONLY WANT TO BROWSE** or I can't find the item I want within my budget, I go to ShopItToMe.com. Much like ShopStyle.com, ShopItToMe.com is an aggregator—but this one hunts only for sale items! The first time you visit, you'll fill out a quick profile where you identify your favorite brands, set your sizes, and pick your discount parameters. Then simply sign up for their sale mail and you'll be notified when your sizes in your favorite brands are discounted.

4. **ANY ONLINE SHOPPING GURU** knows the importance of tracking your packages, and there's no easier way to do this than by using an app called Slice, which "crawls" your in-box looking for

any tracking numbers or online order receipts. It keeps a list of shipping information for all your purchases and notifies you when an item ships or is delivered.

. ● .

When the going gets rough, as it sometimes will, remember: Patience is a virtue, and when it comes to shopping, good deals come to those who wait. If you get discouraged, just remember what you're working toward: a more frugal, more fabulous you. If you lose your way at any point, refer to this list of dos and don'ts for a quick refresher:

Do make a list to help you stay on track when you're shopping.

Don't try to buy everything on the list in one trip.

Do maintain your list as you do seasonal cleanouts, dress daily, and outgrow items.

Don't assume you'll just remember; you've got too much to think about to recall if you've got a black cardigan that fits.

Do push your style beyond its limits from time to time.

Don't end up with a closet full of outliers that you'll never wear.

Do use promotions to your advantage when you really need to buy something.

Don't let tricky sales tactics fool you into buying more than you wanted to.

Do try on everything before you buy it.

Don't assume that just because you've bought from that store before, you know how something will fit.

Do take advantage of markdowns when it's something you love and would pay full price for.

Don't buy something simply because it's at a discount.

Do buy seasonal items during end-of-season sales.

Don't buy seasonal items so trendy that they'll be out of style by the time you can wear them.

Do use web-based resources to help you get the best deal.

Don't get stuck with an item you hate and can't return because you didn't know the return policy.

SPEND VERSUS SAVE *Chapter 5*

I have to be honest about something: I didn't come by my Cheap Chica-ness all by myself. If it wasn't for my mom, a lot of embarrassing financial mistakes in my twenties, and my spreadsheet-loving husband, I might never have become the thrifty fashionista I am today.

A few years ago, I finished a big project that I was really proud of. It was the first time in my career that I had been paid what I considered to be a big—for me—sum of money, and I figured that I deserved a reward for all my hard work (a dangerous feeling I think the Spontaneous Chicas out there can relate to). I decided to spend 10 percent of my paycheck on whatever I wanted. (The 10 percent was completely arbitrary, by the way; I'm sure my husband would have created a spreadsheet to determine a more precise amount.) I went out and bought myself a beautiful necklace . . . *and* a bag *and* a pair of shoes—all of which were on my shopping list, like the one we made in Chapter 4, but nonetheless were still completely unnecessary and irresponsible, considering there were more important things for me to spend my money on.

See, I still had a good deal of student loans left over from school, and while I don't regret a cent I spent on my education, that's where my extra cash should've been allocated. That's what my husband helped me realize: If you have even an iota of debt, any excess money belongs to someone else, be it your credit card company, your mortgage lender, or in my case, my student loan lender.

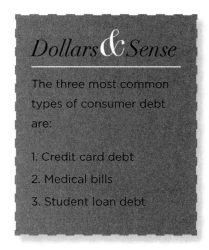

Dollars & Sense

The three most common types of consumer debt are:

1. Credit card debt
2. Medical bills
3. Student loan debt

It took me a few weeks to pull the trigger, but one morning I woke up from my shopping haze and realized how impulsive I'd been. I marched myself back to the store and returned all the things I'd bought—which just goes to show why I've been going on and on about the importance of a flexible return policy!—and mailed a check to my student loan lender the very next morning. It wasn't the glamorous or exciting thing to do, and no one was going to compliment me on paying off my loans like they might've on my handbag, but it was the right way to spend my money and it made me feel better than any bag or shoe ever could. That's when I realized that saving can be sexy! Until my finances were in better shape, I could live with cheap or discounted versions of that necklace, purse, and shoes. Blowing big bucks on high-end items could wait until I was debt-free and had enough extra money to play with. This is a good example of what I call the "save versus spend" theory.

. ● .

The old adage is true: You get what you pay for.

As much as I'd like to believe that there's an exception to this rule, for the most part I've found that whoever coined this phrase was pretty much dead-on. However, I've also found that sometimes, buying a lower-cost item—and in turn getting a lower-quality product— makes sense in certain situations. On the flip side, there are times when it makes sense to spend more money on a top-of-the-line item. Knowing when is the tricky part.

Just as with electronics, cars, food, and just about anything else, the more expensive something is, the nicer the product will be. When it comes to clothes, better brands (and higher prices) mean better fit, fabric, and manufacturing, while bargain brands usually mean sacrificing in one or more areas. If you can afford couture clothing for every occasion, I'd like to thank you for reading this far, Ms. Winfrey, but you can go ahead and set the book down now. That's not who this book was written for. I'm writing for the women who have Balenciaga taste on a Banana Republic budget. And believe it or not, you can get the expensive look you want without spending a fortune. The key is investing *intelligently.*

As we go forward, there are going to be items that I recommend not spending much on (your "save" items), and then there are going to be items that I recommend you spend a little more on (your "spend" items). There's a method to my madness that I promise will become clear as we go on. And bear in mind: I'm only asking you to buy the best you can afford, not what someone else can afford.

No matter how much advice I dole out in these pages, it's up to you, and only you, to honestly assess your financial situation and decide what exactly a "spend" means to you. Perhaps your status quo is Nordstrom, and an investment piece comes from Neiman Marcus. Or maybe at this point in your life, you're exclusively an H&M girl and a "spend" means a visit to J.Crew. Wherever you stand, it's important that you invest at a price point that's comfortable and manageable for you. There's no shame in shopping within your means—in fact, it's something to be quite proud of, and let's face it: It sure beats the embarrassment of calls from collectors. No shoes are worth financial ruin.

Over the course of this chapter, we're going to assess the difference between quality and quantity, and I'll outline which items you should spend on and which items are appropriate to save on. I'll also teach you the details that set off "cheap!" alarms so that even if you save on something, the whole world doesn't have to know it. Once you're armed with this information, you'll be able to curate the right mix of high- and low-end items so that neither your closet nor your bank account suffers.

QUALITY VERSUS QUANTITY

Let's imagine a little scenario: It's payday (hurrah!) and you've got $400 to spend on clothes for the month. You go to the mall and you see a fabulous Alice and Olivia dress for $395. You love it, but you decide to keep looking before spending your entire clothing allowance at once. You head into H&M, where you find an assortment of thirteen tops, skirts, and pants for an average of $30 each. You've encountered the ultimate shopping conundrum: Do you spend nearly $400 on a single item, or do you get thirteen pieces that add up to the same amount?

[
WOMAN CANNOT LIVE ON QUALITY OR QUANTITY ALONE.
]

In other words, the question you're really asking yourself is this: Should I go for quality or quantity? There are positives and negatives to both choices. If you choose the single high-quality item, you'll have a piece that will last you for years—but one garment isn't enough to make weeks' worth of outfits with. If you choose the thirteen $30 pieces, on the other hand, you'll have lots of clothes to mix and match (and don't forget to check out The Lucky 13 in the photo insert to see just how far these thirteen pieces can stretch)—but they might all be threadbare by next season.

Clearly, woman cannot live on quality or quantity alone. The key is to find the right balance.

WHAT'S THE RIGHT BALANCE FOR ME?

O f course, we'd all love to have a closet full of only the finest high-end designer items, but unless you're Beyoncé or you're married to Bill Gates, that's probably not realistic. At the same time, you don't want everything you own to have come from the clearance rack at Charlotte Russe, or you'll need to replace everything in your closet at the end of each season. But finding a balance isn't the same for everyone—some of us can and should lean more in one direction or the other, depending on lifestyle and needs. See where you fall on the scale below:

Quality Focus

You should invest mostly in quality items if you . . .

. . . work in a conservative environment where style is of less importance than looking put together and professional. The same simple black suit could last for your entire climb up the corporate ladder, so you'll want to buy one that will make it there with you.

. . . are over forty. The older you get, the less you should be concerned with trends and the more you should focus on the style that you've identified as your own over the years. If you start off purchasing a few investment pieces each year when you're young, by the time you reach middle age, you'll have a wardrobe full of fad-proof, high-quality items that will keep you looking like the timeless beauty you are.

Equal Balance

You require an equal amount of quality and quantity items if you . . .

. . . need to strike a balance between practicality and presentation. Maybe you're a teacher who needs her clothes to withstand multiple wears and washes but you're on a limited budget. You'll want a wardrobe with a mix of price points and quality for your varying needs.

. . . are a young professional just starting out. No one would expect you to have an Armani pantsuit in your repertoire, though it's good to start investing in pieces now that will last long past your next promotion. On the weekends, though, you're still painting the town red, so you'll need some trendier clothes to see and be seen in.

Quantity Focus

It makes sense for you to spend on lower-quality items if you . . .

. . . work in an alternative field like the hospitality industry, music, or the arts. Whatever it is, your lifestyle requires a hipper slant than most others. Since you can't afford to be constantly changing out an entire designer wardrobe every season, it's best to go for bargains.

. . . are in the marketing, advertising, or social media fields, in which your livelihood depends on your ability to stay up-to-date on what's trending in pop culture. Being current is crucial to your success, and you'll want your wardrobe to reflect that. Just make sure you don't go broke trying to look trendy—that's definitely not on anyone's hot list.

. . . are a new mom. Between dodging spit-up stains and playing in the yard, your clothes suffer a lot of abuse. There's no sense in spending a lot on a suede jacket that's just going to be sent to the dry cleaner an hour after you put it on. Opt for lower-priced, sensible sportswear.

SPEND VERSUS SAVE

N ow that we've dissected the concept of quality versus quantity, you should understand why it's important to spend more money on some things but less on others. But what kinds of items should you be willing to *spend* on, and where should you embrace your inner cheapskate and *save*? Let's examine the when and why of each.

Spend

Generally, you want to spend on investment pieces, which, for the most part, are going to fall under the "Basics" category that we outlined in Chapter 3 (see page 102). Why? Because well-made basics will last you for years, in terms of both wear-and-tear and style. You could skimp on your staples, but then you'll just have to replace them a lot more often. Or you could max out your budget on a high-quality pair of neon pumps, but who's going to want to wear them three years from now (even though they'll still be in great shape)? To get the most mileage out of your money, "spends" should occur at the intersection of timelessness and quality.

"Spends" should:

be thought through. Just as with any other type of investment, expensive clothes shouldn't be impulse buys.

be budgeted for. When you see something you want, start saving for it. Buy it once you've got enough socked away. Resist the urge to put it on a credit card and pay for it after the fact.

add value to your style through wearability. Anything you purchase should go with at least three other items in your closet to make it worthwhile. An investment piece should match five things at minimum.

give you that indefinable "I feel so much better with it" feeling. Sometimes, the right piece can transform you, in which case, a purchase is justifiable. (Just be careful that you don't get that feeling with every piece you try on.)

One of my best "spends" has to be the pair of Christian Louboutin nude Pigalle pumps that I bought in 2007 for $400 using a friend's Barney's New York discount. Though $400 is certainly beyond my typical spending comfort level, I knew I'd get tons of wear out of them—and I was right. I've had them for six years now and I still wear them constantly. The neutral color goes with everything, and thanks to the almond toe shape, which isn't too pointy or too rounded, they never go out of style. And like any good fashionista does with her investment purchases, I take care of them to give them a longer life. I've had them resoled three times, and I keep the toes stuffed when I'm not wearing them so that they don't crease.

Let's get specific. Here are some types of garments that are acceptable to spend on:

- **SPEND** on something you'll get a lot of wear out of. Depending on what you do for a living and how you spend your free time, that could mean a smart suit or a Tumi carry-on if you travel a ton.

- **SPEND** on timeless items. Staples like the ones on the list on pages 103–105 are worth the investment.

- **SPEND** on nice denim. I love J Brand jeans, which cost nearly $200—a tough price for me to swallow. But not only do I wear them on a regular basis; no other jeans make my butt look better, and since I buy them in an inky dark wash, they look good with just about any top in my closet.

- **SPEND** on things that fit you like a glove. An item that is perfectly tailored instantly looks expensive.

- **SPEND** on classic colors. While a wardrobe of black, white, gray, and tan may not sound thrilling, neutral shades like these are timeless and will be just as popular fifteen years from now as they are today. You can spice up a neutral outfit with a splash of color here and there.

- **SPEND** on quality materials and high-quality construction. Not sure how to determine an item's quality? Turn to page 194, where I'll spill the giveaways of cheap construction.

- **SPEND** on outerwear. If chosen wisely, one good coat could be all you need for a few seasons.

- **SPEND** on shoes in universal colors and styles, like a nude pump and a black ballet flat. There is nothing more luxurious than a well-made shoe. More expensive brands are easier on the foot and last longer when given the proper care.

- **SPEND** on a handbag in a neutral color. One fabulous bag beats a collection of plastic-looking purses any day. I've got a thick pebble-leather Marc by Marc Jacobs tote in burgundy-brown that I've had for seven years that barely has any scratches or damage. I've also recently started a love affair with Céline hand-bags. I love how they blend classic styles with fashion-forward details and functionality. Over the last three years, I've splurged on one in black and tan and another in dark gray.

- **SPEND** on a nice wristwatch. Too many people rely on their cell phones to give them the time. Even though I'm usually a proponent of saving on jewelry, I believe that a classic watch is worth a little extra cash. I splurged on a Rolex in the most timeless (no pun intended) look I could find: Roman numerals on a white face with a stainless steel bracelet. Even when I'm stressed for time, looking down at my watch brings a smile to my face!

- **SPEND** on camisoles. I think camisoles are a great investment piece. Considering how much we wear and wash them, I believe it's worth it to spend a little bit more money ($20 versus $10) to get one made of a much better fabric and with better-quality construction.

- **SPEND** on quality undergarments. These create the foundation that the rest of your clothes will lie on. If a bra cuts into your back or gapes in the front, it's not fitted properly and will distract from even the most gorgeous outfit. It's worth it to buy pieces that enhance your individual shape and lay discreetly underneath your clothes.

If you find a garment so perfect it was as though the style gods sent it down from heaven just for you, but the price is more than you can justify, use these tips:

- **WAIT FOR A SALE.** Try prodding the sales associate for information about if and when that item will go on markdown. Then check back—and often!

- **TRY BARGAINING.** Depending on what type of store you're in, there may be wiggle room in the asking price. Consignment stores in particular are usually willing to negotiate—this is one of my favorite ways to score designer deals!

Dollars & Sense

Revamping your wardrobe shouldn't be an overnight project. Treat yourself to one or two investment pieces each year. You'll slowly build up a wardrobe of great go-to garments that you can wear until you're eighty.

- **USE A COUPON.** Many stores send out coupons to customers who are a part of their loyalty programs. Sign up for mailings and e-mail blasts to take advantage of such offers, or check a mall's visitor center, which often has coupons available.

- **CALCULATE THE COST PER WEAR.** While you should never spend more than you're comfortable with, it's helpful to calculate the estimated cost per wear of an item by dividing the cost by the number of times you expect to wear it. The more you wear something, the "cheaper" it becomes. If you were to wear a pair of $150 jeans every day for a year, the cost per wear would be $0.41. On the contrary, if you spent $30 on a pair you didn't love and ended up wearing them only twice, the cost per wear would be a much less reasonable $15.

Dollars & Sense

What should you aim for when considering cost per wear? I think a good margin is $5—anything with a CPW of that or less is a great deal!

- **BE LOYAL.** Take advantage of loyalty-program savings that high-end department stores like Bloomingdale's, Neiman Marcus, Saks Fifth Avenue, and Nordstrom offer, in which you receive points for every dollar you spend and are rewarded with gift cards when you reach a certain points total.

> THE MORE YOU WEAR SOMETHING,
> THE "CHEAPER" IT BECOMES.

Save

Now we've come to the part of the chapter that makes a Cheap Chica like me really happy: saving! There is no greater satisfaction than being asked where you got something you're wearing and getting to share the amazing backstory behind an incredible find. I've had many of these stories over the years, but one in particular takes the cake.

I have always considered myself an equal-opportunity shopper. I will shop anywhere, anytime—no questions asked. That explains how I ended up in a shop in Philadelphia called Expressions. At first sight, it's the kind of place that might make you blush, with some rather racy outfits hanging in the window (and by "outfits," I mean small strips of fabric that cover the essentials). Let's just say, it was far from J.Crew. But being the open-minded shopper that I am, I looked past the "outfits" to where I could see rows of shoes in the back of the store.

I threw a quick glance over my shoulder to make sure no one I knew was within eyesight, and when I was sure the coast was clear, I darted into the store. I walked past racks of neon bandage "dresses," rows of sequin "shorts," and tons of skintight "pants" when I noticed a table piled high with denim. On closer inspection, I found that these were the perfect dark skinny jeans: soft, simple stitching, inky dark-blue wash, clean pockets, 2 percent Lycra, and a just-right rise, very similar to my beloved J Brand jeans. I tried them on in a makeshift dressing room (read: behind a hastily hung curtain) and lo and behold, they fit my petite frame perfectly. Best of all, they were marked at $20 apiece—and were buy-one-get-one-half-off!

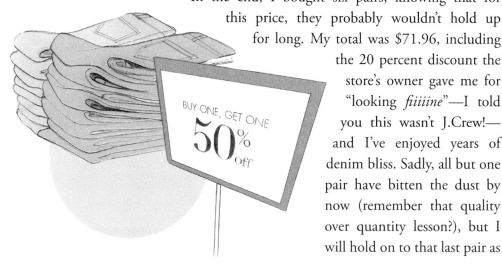

In the end, I bought six pairs, knowing that for this price, they probably wouldn't hold up for long. My total was $71.96, including the 20 percent discount the store's owner gave me for "looking *fiiiine*"—I told you this wasn't J.Crew!—and I've enjoyed years of denim bliss. Sadly, all but one pair have bitten the dust by now (remember that quality over quantity lesson?), but I will hold on to that last pair as long as I possibly can. Since then, Expressions has become one of my go-to stores for frugal footwear, which is what drew me into the store in the first place. The moral of this story? Never judge a book by its cover—or a store by its questionable window displays.

You don't have to go scouring your city for hidden finds like this one—there are plenty of good deals to be had at stores that you already know. It's not where you shop that matters—it's being savvy and persistent enough to find the best "saves" the store has to offer and not being swayed by retailers' tricks to spend more than you're comfortable with.

Why is this so crucial? Because buying "save" items helps us achieve the balance that I said earlier was so important. Since the items we save on tend to be more expendable with season or wear and tear, it makes sense to buy low on the following pieces:

- **SAVE** on things that get replaced often, like socks, and hosiery. Hosiery snags and stretches after a season of wearing, so I toss and replace mine regularly.

- **SAVE** on jewelry. With jewelry trends having such a short shelf life, it's better to rely on discount shops like Forever 21 for your flashier pieces. There are exceptions: I, for instance, have a weakness for Hermès bracelets, many of which have been gifts from my husband. Timeless pieces like these are worth the investment. But the majority of my jewelry pieces are quantity purchases, often costing $10 or less.

- **SAVE** on belts. I wear belts three to four times a week. I use them to cinch in shapeless frocks or to make a simple item look more sophisticated—but I rarely spend more than $10 on one. The

Think you won't regret an expensive "now" purchase later? Let's remember some of the worst trends in recent history to prove that trends aren't for splurging on:

• Baby backpacks
• Scrunchies
• Fanny packs
• Harem pants
• Fingerless gloves
• Visible thongs
• Leg warmers
• Trucker hats
• Velour jumpsuits
• Overalls

thickness, body placement, material, and color trends change so often that they're not worth dropping a lot of money on.

• **SAVE** on trends. You'll be glad you didn't spend a lot on them when you're donating them to Goodwill after a year.

• **SAVE** on brightly colored items. Aside from neutrals and other classic shades, colors come in and out of style quickly, and you don't want to be stuck with expensive jeans in the color of the season—two seasons later.

• **SAVE** on sparkle. You know that sequin dress that's perfect for New Year's Eve? Well, that's just about the only thing it's perfect for. Special-occasion items like that are best saved on, since the cost per wear is extremely high.

• **SAVE** on your outliers. Those items that don't fit into your everyday lifestyle don't warrant a high price tag. While it's acceptable to have a few of these out-of-left-field pieces, they shouldn't be expensive for the same reasons your special-occasion garments shouldn't—the cost per wear ends up being too great.

• **SAVE** on synthetic fabrics like polyester, rayon, nylon, spandex, and acrylics. These aren't high-quality fabrics that are worth hanging on to.

- **SAVE** on swimwear. Your bathing suit gets exposed to a lot of abuse from sun (and sunscreen, natch), sand, saltwater, and chlorine. A shorter-than-average shelf life is inevitable when a piece of clothing gets put through that much, so don't blow a bunch of money on a big-name bikini. Instead, buy basic separates that can be mixed and matched to get the most looks for the least cash. For the best deals, shop at the end of summer and save the suit for next beach season.

The Cheap Chica's Cheat Sheet

For quick reference, here's a handy guide on when to *spend* and when to *save*:

SPEND

Things that will get lots of wear

Timeless pieces

Nice denim

Garments that fit like a glove

Classic colors

Quality materials and construction

Outerwear

Shoes in universal colors and styles

Handbags in neutral colors

Camisoles

Watch

Undergarments

Things that get replaced often (socks, hosiery, etc.)

Jewelry

Belts

Trends

Brightly colored items

Sparkly items

Outliers

Synthetic fabrics

Swimwear

BARGAIN VERSUS CHEAP

While we're talking about saving, there's an important distinction I want to make sure you're aware of: There's a difference between a bargain item and a just plain cheap item. A *bargain* is an article of clothing that is made well, is constructed of quality materials, fits properly without gathering or pulling, and comes at a great price. Something that's *cheap* is made from low-quality fabric, is poorly executed, and doesn't flatter your body—and that's regardless of the price. When I say *cheap* in this case, I'm talking less about price and more about quality, as there are cheap clothes that cost $5 and cheap clothes that cost $100. (Side note: This is the only time you'll hear me use *cheap* as a bad word!)

Luckily, it's easy to tell the difference between a bargain and cheap clothes if you know what to look for:

Buttons

- **SHINY VERSUS MATTE OR COVERED.** Avoid shiny buttons whenever possible. The coating that manufacturers use to give buttons that sheen is cheap and often flakes off with wear and washing. Matte or covered buttons are a sign of higher quality.

- **OPERABLE BUTTONS AT THE CUFF OF A JACKET VERSUS NO BUTTONS AT ALL.** Operable buttons instantly add value, as each buttonhole must be cut and sewn individually.

Color

- **RICH AND SATURATED VERSUS LIGHTER.** Though it's natural to think that more color equals better quality, fabric plays a big role in what shades look best. Silks, charmeuse, organza, and crepe de chine look best (read: expensive) in soft shades. Poly blends, on the other hand, look more chic in rich, saturated colors.

Fabric

- **NATURAL VERSUS SYNTHETIC.** I think natural-fiber fabrics like wool, silk, cotton, and linen always trump synthetic fabrics like nylon, polyester, and acetate, which can lean toward looking cheap. Pay attention to fabrics and, when you can, opt for natural ones, which will last longer and launder more easily.

Style Cents

Though having operable buttons at the cuff is a sign of quality, it can make shortening sleeves nearly impossible for a tailor. Before you buy, determine how much length you'd need removed from the cuff and see where the new hem would be in relation to the buttons.

Patterns

- **ALIGNED VERSUS UNALIGNED.** Items of quality manufacturing will have patterns or prints that line up along the seams. Cheap items won't.

Seams

- **TIGHT VERSUS LOOSE.** On quality items, the stitching on a seam will be relatively tight, though not so tight as to pucker or constrict the fabric. Serged seams (on knit fabrics only) or double-straight seams are typically stronger than a simple single-straight seam and therefore a

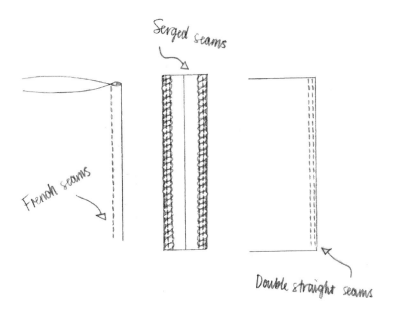

Serged seams

French seams

Double straight seams

sign of quality. Cheaper items might have loosely stitched seams, seams that are too tight, or broken stitches.

- **FRENCH VERSUS SERGED.** Serged seams—made when fabric is pressed through a serger, then stitched and cut simultaneously—are a low-quality solution on anything but knit fabrics. On the other hand, a French seam means that each seam has been stitched twice to ensure that it doesn't break with wear and tear—a sure sign of quality construction.

Hem Allowance

- **GENEROUS HEM VERSUS VIRTUALLY NO HEM.** Cheap clothes will have hems that were serged and sewn with very minimal hem allowance, while quality items are serged, then sewn discreetly with a hem allowance of several inches, enabling you to lengthen a garment.

Style Cents

As practical as functional pockets are, sometimes they can gape open on the sides of pants—making you look wider—or an interior pocket can give you a case of lumpy butt, which is never attractive. Your tailor can help by stitching the pocket openings shut, or, if you're handy with a pair of scissors, you can remove back pockets yourself. Removing the interior pockets on a pair of white jeans is also a must so they don't show through the white fabric.

Lining and Reinforcement

• **LINING VERSUS NO LINING.** Look for fabric reinforcements such as facing (lining around the edge or around delicate areas of a garment), as this can greatly increase the value of a piece of clothing. Also check to see if the item is fully lined, which will make it last longer and wear better.

Pockets

• **FUNCTIONAL VERSUS FAUX.** Inspect the pockets to see how well they've been finished, as this is typically a good indicator of the quality of workmanship. A faux pocket is usually a sign that shortcuts were taken in manufacturing. Remember: Some pockets come sewn shut, so don't assume it's not a functioning pocket if you can't force your hand inside. Look inside the item to check for a pocket allowance.

Zippers

- **METAL VERSUS PLASTIC.** Aside from buttons, zippers are the most-used detail on clothing, showing up regularly on dresses, pants, shorts, tops, outerwear, shoes, and accessories. The type of zipper used is typically determined by the weight of the fabric; the heavier the fabric, the more durable a zipper you're going to need. With lighter fabrics like nylons, polyester blends, cottons, and Lycra, you can get away with a plastic closure, while heavier materials such as denim, leather, canvas, and wool usually require a more substantial metal version.

- **EXPOSED VERSUS INVISIBLE.** Though exposed zippers have seen a recent resurgence, that's a trendier look than the classic invisible zipper, which is found primarily on eveningwear and dress clothes. Invisible zippers are hidden within the seams of a garment to leave a clean finish when zipped closed. An elegant dress tends to look much more expensive with this type of zipper.

Boning

- **BONING VERSUS NO BONING.** Boning is used to help a garment maintain its shape and to give support under a close-fitting dress or top. You'll find this feature on a lot of high-quality formal wear, as well as corset-style tops and some swimwear.

Embellishments

- **SEWN ON VERSUS ADHESIVE.** Pay attention to how embellishments such as sequins, studs, grommets, beads, and rhinestones are applied to your garment. Higher-quality items will have them individually sewn on, whereas cheaper variations will be adhered with glue.

Hardware

- **HARDWARE VERSUS NO HARDWARE.** In terms of quality, heavy metal hardware beats plastic faux replicas, hands down. Not only are the embellishments themselves of a better quality, but the fabric they're attached to must also be substantial to support their weight, adding to the overall value.

Elastic

- **EXPOSED VERSUS TUNNELED.** Exposed elastic is most often seen at the waistline of a skirt, usually in a basic black or white. Tunneled elastic, however, is fed through the waistband so it's not visible to the naked eye. Neither of these options, which are used to fit the most people with the least amount of work, is preferable to a tailored waist with a zipper.

Distress

- **PRESENT VERSUS NOT.** The purpose of "distress details" on a material like denim or leather is to give the item a broken-in appearance. This preworn look can actually increase the cost of a garment, as counterintuitive as it may seem, simply because it required extra steps in the manufacturing process, such as sanding or rewashing.

SHOE GUIDE

Material

Feel the fabric with your hands; is it rough to the touch, or does it look shiny and plasticlike? Does the shoe cut into your foot? If you answer yes to either of these questions, put that pair back and keep on walking. When shopping for bargain shoes, look for matte fabrics that mimic the look of real leather and suede. This rule applies when shopping for budget handbags, as well. If it looks fake to you, it will look fake to others. Wait until you find something worth parting with your cash for.

Hardware

Opt for matte finishes on any hardware; just as with the coating on cheap buttons, the shiny mock finish on cheap metal will flake off with time. The same goes for handbags, on which plastic zippers should also be avoided, as they instantly make something look low budget.

Construction

Do you feel any sharp thread edges poking at your foot? Notice glue overspill peeking out from between the sole and the upper? Is the stitching crooked? These are all signs that a shoe was constructed on the cheap. Wear with caution.

· ● ·

While I know temptation is all around, rest assured that an eye for detail and an understanding of when to spend and when to save will leave you with long-lasting and cost-efficient style. Resist the urge to buy just for the sake of buying—it will lead only to a closet you can't stand in a matter of months. Smart shopping leads to satisfied dressing.

Now that you know what to save on, you'll need to know *how* and *where* to find the best deals. In the next chapter, I'll teach you just that.

[
RESIST THE URGE TO BUY JUST FOR
THE SAKE OF BUYING—IT WILL LEAD ONLY
TO A CLOSET YOU CAN'T STAND
IN A MATTER OF MONTHS.
]

THE ART OF

OF *Chapter 6*

THE

STEAL

I'm no good with a paintbrush and a canvas, and I can't write you a song, but I truly believe that style is an art form, so I consider myself an artist in my own right! It takes a creative spirit and an eye for detail to put together a great-looking outfit. Having the vision to see the potential in a pair of thrift-store ankle boots and the imagination to pair them with a lacy shift from T.J.Maxx makes you as much an artist as any impressionist painter.

What I wear is an outward expression of how I'm feeling or what I'm going through. You know how artists' and singers' work is often classified by periods? I can totally go back through old pictures and remember where I was in my life based on what I was wearing. First, there was my "corporate chic" period, when I moved to New York at age twenty-two and wore tons of pencil skirts to work because I thought they made me look grown-up and sophisticated. When I moved to Philadelphia and started my blog in 2007, I was working from home and really sad about leaving New York. Consequently, I spent way too much time in leggings, so I'll call that my "stretchy-chic" era. Now that my schedule is a mix of working from home, traveling for work, and making regular appearances on television, my wardrobe sometimes feels like it belongs to two people. This would be my "bipolar" era. I'm either totally glammed out for TV (we're talking full makeup and extensions) or relaxed but put together so I can go to meetings with clients but still travel to and from New York comfortably.

> BEING AWARE OF ALL YOUR OPTIONS IS THE BEST WAY TO BUILD AN ARTISTIC WARDROBE THAT BALANCES STYLE AND SAVVY.

And even from day to day, there's a subtle difference in my style. Most days, I'm a girly girl, but every once in a while, I get the urge to edge up my look, and the right jacket can accomplish that! That, Chicas, is called artistic expression.

For this reason, I think people should take pride in the way they look, and even in the way they shop. And while your inspirations may change from year to year, or even from week to week, I want you to always have the power and know-how to buy whatever it is that best expresses you at that moment for a price that works within your lifestyle. To that end, I'm going to share with you my secrets on the art of the "steal."

In the following pages, I'll discuss the ins and outs of retailers, outlets, secondhand stores, and websites that will help you look chic for cheap. I'll explain the benefits of each,

share how I prefer to approach them, and give you specific ones to try. Essentially, this chapter will be your all-encompassing reference guide to every *what, where,* and *how* I know of to find a bargain! Being aware of all your options is the best way to build an artistic wardrobe that balances style and savvy.

RETAILERS

There are a million stores out there, each eager to take your money in exchange for their garments. But all stores are not created equal. Certain types of retailers lend themselves to budget shopping better than others. Here's a breakdown of the best places to save and why.

Fast-Fashion Stores

Fast-fashion stores have completely changed the way we shop. Because they offer their goods at such low prices, we can afford to dabble in different styles and try out trends we ordinarily might not. While you wouldn't want to fill an entire closet with finds from these stores, they're great for temporarily bridging gaps in your wardrobe and helping you explore your style.

Forever 21. This fast-growing chain offers trendy threads at unbelievably low prices. The quality suffers a bit, but purchases made here should be seen as disposable—they're likely to be out of style as the threads are starting to give out, anyway!

- *Great for:* Trends and accessories
- *Online shopping available?* Yes (www .forever21.com)
- *Look out for:* Their Love 21 section—the cuts are more generous and the styles have a more sophisticated, grown-up feel.
- *Note:* Forever 21 accepts exchanges only for store credit for up to twenty-one days with receipt; jewelry and sale items are final sales. If you shop online, you can get a full refund if you return via mail.

H&M. This Swedish import is the more grown-up version of Forever 21, selling fashion-forward clothes at reasonable prices. Construction is typically better than that in other stores of a similar concept, and designers often release limited runs of garments exclusive to H&M.

- *Great for:* Structured basics, casual work clothes, runway-inspired trends, blazers, skirts, jewelry, and denim
- *Online shopping available?* No
- *Look out for:* The tags inside your garments. H&M has several labels ranging from more basic, affordable clothes (Divided by H&M) to more elevated,

Now You Know

Tips for shopping at Forever 21:

1. Unlike most stores, Forever 21 won't sell you the merchandise that's on the mannequins. They can, however, put these items on hold and notify you when they're available for purchase.

2. Each section of the store is divided into styles, so if you're a boho-chic girl, most of what you'll like will be primarily in one area. (Though as ransacked as this place gets, garments can end up all over the place.)

3. That leads to my last tip: Go early! Your best shot for finding the sizes and styles you want is to go first thing in the morning, when the stores are still organized.

designer-inspired pieces (H&M). I tend to shop the H&M label since it feels and looks more luxe.

Zara.   Thanks to a lightning-fast production cycle, Zara is able to copy the top looks off the runway and have imitation versions in the store within weeks. It's one of the pricier of the fast-fashion concept stores, but with styles so current, it's still a steal over designer alternatives. Plus, you can almost always find something great on sale.

- *Great for:* Shoes, trends, coats and jackets, blouses, colorful separates, blazers, and belts
- *Online shopping available?* Yes (www.zara.com)
- *Look out for:* The TRF label. Just like at H&M, there are several labels under the Zara umbrella. TRF is the younger sister to the Zara collection and prices are typically under $50. Look for it in the back of the store.

Charlotte Russe.   Yes, your fifteen-year-old cousin may shop here, but that doesn't mean you can't, too. Over the last few years, the brand has really upped its style game, and you can find great pieces (mixed in with some not-so-age-appropriate styles). You just have to take the time to look.

- *Great for:* Shoes, jewelry, and jeans (especially if you're petite)
- *Online shopping available?* Yes (www.charlotterusse.com)
- *Look out for:* Their BOGO online shoe sales. While they carry some questionable styles at times, they do have a great selection of (mostly) on-trend shoes!

The Art of the Steal: Fast-Fashion Stores

While stores billed as "fast fashion" can be great for scoring up-to-date looks at below-market prices, the quality isn't always top-notch. Here's how to avoid looking like you went rummaging through the bargain bin:

Stick to basic cuts and shapes that are forgiving rather than formfitting. The closer the fit, the better the tailoring ought to be for the garment to look chic.

Look for details that add—not subtract—from the look. Glued-on embellishments are a no; metal buckles or buttons are a yes (as long as they're in a tempered finish that won't crack or peel). Piping, operable buttons, and contrasting collars can make an item look more expensive than it really is, since those are details usually reserved for higher-quality products.

When shopping for leather look-alikes, choose natural hues in the brown or black family to avoid selecting a garment that looks obviously fake.

Pay attention to logos. If an item has a pattern that's intended to look like a designer's calling card—but it's even a hair off—that's a dead giveaway. You want your look to be *inspired* by the designers, not like you're trying to rip them off.

Off-Price Department Stores

I am a big believer in the power of off-price shopping. The thrill of the hunt at stores like these really gives me a shopper's high, and the gratification when I find something amazing is indescribable. Unfortunately, temptation abounds at stores like these because they carry so much more than just clothes. Because my love for clothes is rivaled only by my love for interior design, even a pro like me can get distracted by all the throw pillows, candles, mirrors, art, and glassware at these stores. When you're shopping for clothes, the key is to keep your eyes on the prize.

Style Cents

My shopping strategy at discount stores is much the same as in department stores:

1. Grab a cart and head straight to the clearance section in the back.
2. Shop for dresses.
3. Shop for separates.
4. Edit before going into the dressing room, not at the rack. (At stores like these, if you don't grab it, someone else will! So put everything you respond to in your cart; then decide later what will go into the dressing room with you.)
5. Try your selections on.
6. Look at shoes.
7. Shop for accessories.
8. Check out. (And try to not get distracted by point-of-sale items in line!)

T.J.Maxx. I can't get enough of T.J.Maxx. They have great deals on just about anything you could imagine—including coveted high-end brands!

- *Great for:* Dresses, shoes, and designer denim
- *Online shopping available?* No
- *Look out for:* Many locations have a Runway section, which is my favorite T.J.Maxx feature. There you can find high-quality designer garments at slashed prices. I've found Alice and Olivia, Prada, Louboutin, and Rag & Bone in Runway sections at different stores across the country.

> ## Fashion Fact
>
> I love shopping at T.J.Maxx, and with good reason: 85 percent of store merchandise is guaranteed to be in season, while less than 5 percent of the inventory in most T.J.Maxx stores is imperfect.

Loehmann's. This discount retailer offers garments at 30 to 65 percent off regular price. Their "back room" features fantastic designer names at double-digit discounts. Though stores are found in only eleven states, you can still shop no matter where you live thanks to their thorough online store.

- *Great for:* Separates, jackets, and casual basics
- *Online shopping available?* Yes (www.loehmanns.com)

Marshalls. This national off-price retailer carries a great selection of home goods and kitchenware in addition to discounted clothes and, best of all, a renowned shoe department.

- *Great for:* Shoes, jeans, blouses, and belts
- *Online shopping available?* No

[ ]

The Art of the Steal: Off-Price Stores

Discount retailers bring out the wild side in women—we go into survival mode, unafraid to snatch clothes out from under other women's noses in the name of saving money. This means stores are often in disarray and merchandise heavily picked over. To succeed at this type of store, keep these tips in mind:

1. Go early. When shopping at off-price retailers, the early bird gets the worm! Each store gets a limited number of pieces in, and once they're gone, they're gone. So if you love something, get it!

2. Go often. These stores put new merchandise out several times a week, so every time you come back, it'll be like a whole new store.

3. Avoid the crowds. During the week, when most people are working, I head to stores in the suburbs, which are bound to be less crowded. On weekends, when the worker bees are resting at home, I'll venture to a downtown location. Fewer people mean cleaner stores, better selection, and shorter lines.

4. Consider the demographic. If you're shopping at a store located in a young, hip part of town, the trendier garments in desirable sizes may go quickly. If you find this happening, seek out other locations in parts of town with a different clientele so you've got a better shot at snagging what you want.

5. Make friends with the store manager and ask him or her to contact you when pieces by your favorite designers come in. That way you'll get first dibs!

Big-Box Stores

Plentiful, affordable, accessible—big-box stores sure make it hard not to love them. The trick to shopping at stores like these is to focus only on items that can pass as expensive and to not fall for every low price you see, no matter what it's attached to. Remember, we're trying to look chic for cheap, not just plain cheap. Here are some of my favorites:

How It Works: Diffusion Line

A diffusion line is a clothing collection by a high-end designer that sells at a lower price point than the designer's primary line. This practice expands the reach of designer labels, allowing access for people who ordinarily couldn't afford such luxuries.

Shoppers should be aware, however, that the quality of big-box-store diffusion lines is not the same as that for true designer labels. While the garments may reflect the vision of the designer, often the only real similarity between the lines is the name on the tag. While I love diffusion lines, I recommend never spending more than $50 on a diffusion-line piece, as the quality doesn't warrant any more than that.

Another important thing to realize is that the clothing lines you see that are "designed" by celebrities—the Kardashian Kollection at Sears, Miley Cyrus for Walmart, and Jennifer Lopez for Kohl's, for example—are a different thing entirely. In these cases, the celebrities may have inspired the pieces or assisted the designer with curating the collection, but most times they simply *(continued)* lend their name to the collection, participate in the marketing and promotion of the brand, and profit from the sales. It's an extremely lucrative business—Selena Gomez, for instance, reportedly made more than $100 million on her Dream Out Loud collection with Kmart—but don't be fooled into thinking you're really getting a dress designed by your favorite star.

Target.   I can't really think of anything that I don't love to buy at Target, but in recent years, the omnipresent chain has really stepped up its fashion game, bringing in designers to create "diffusion lines" (see How It Works: Diffusion Line, on the previous page) that have proven incredibly popular. (The Missoni for Target line, for instance, crashed the retailer's website and sold out within hours.) In-store brands like Mossimo and Merona produce passable imitations of popular looks at great prices.

- *Great for:* Basic tees and tanks, diffusion lines and designer-inspired looks, swimwear, and sandals
- *Online shopping available?* Yes (www.target.com)
- *Look out for:* The red clearance stickers and clearance sections at the back of each aisle, where you can really save big!
- *Note:* Returns are welcome for up to ninety days after purchase on most items with a receipt; stores offer receipt lookup if you don't have the original invoice.

Kohl's.   Kohl's offers permanent celebrity/designer brands such as LC Lauren Conrad, the Jennifer Lopez collection, and Simply Vera by Vera Wang, which up the store's fashion quotient by a significant margin.

- *Great for:* Trends on the cheap, particularly the LC Lauren Conrad and Simply Vera collections, undergarments, scarves, and cardigans

- *Online shopping available?* Yes (www.kohls.com)
- *Look out for:* The store's excellent Kohl's Cash program, which gives you $10 cash back to use on future purchases (with no minimum amount) for every $50 you spend in the store.
- *Note:* No time restriction on returns.

JCP. This isn't your grandmother's J.C. Penney! The store has totally reinvented itself, eschewing the full-length name for a hipper acronym and introducing designer and celebrity lines.

- *Great for:* Dresses, sandals, hats, and jeans
- *Online shopping available?* Yes (www.jcpenney.com)
- *Look out for:* Some stores now have a Sephora shop inside, so you can pick up a new shade of blush while you shop for a blouse. And don't skip the juniors' section—they have great-fitting denim ranging in size from 00 to 13!
- *Note:* No time restriction on returns.

[ ]

Midsize Retailers

There are plenty of options at your average mall that won't rake you over the financial coals. Whatever your taste—boho-chic, ultra-fem, preppy to the max—there's a budget-friendly store to suit your needs. The following stores are some of my favorites; they offer lots of top-notch sales for even greater savings.

Urban Outfitters. Don't let the emaciated hipster kids in the catalogs intimidate you—their merchandise, while a bit on the younger side, is more forgiving than it looks. Regular prices are a tad high for what you get, so it's best to wait for sales, which are generous and frequent.

- *Great for:* Dresses, trendy tops, pretty underwear, and funky accessories
- *Online shopping available?* Yes (www.urbanoutfitters.com)
- *Look out for:* Their sale e-mails! You'll have prime access to the best selection before the most sought-after sizes and colors are gone.

Anthropologie. Every woman's favorite store to waste hours in (and every man's worst nightmare) can also be one of the more overpriced. Don't ever spend top dollar on garments there—sales are plentiful and well worth the wait. When you go between sales, head straight for the back room, where the clearance items are.

- *Great for:* Feminine tops and dresses, forgiving pants, and statement jewelry
- *Online shopping available?* Yes (www.anthropologie.com)
- *Look out for:* Their new petite sizes for us smaller gals!

- **Note:** Returns welcome indefinitely, with or without receipt; price adjustments given within fourteen days of purchase

Banana Republic. Classic and conservative, Banana Republic is always reliable for smart-casual and work clothes as well as timeless dresses, shoes, and jewelry. Sales abound in store and online, and coupons are given out frequently in store and via snail mail and e-mail, so be sure to sign up for all their mailing lists to get the best deals.

- **Great for:** Staples, work clothes, and leather bags
- **Online shopping available?** Yes (www.bananarepublic.com)

LOFT. Ann Taylor's little sister is all grown up and now a full-fledged member of the fashion family. Offering smart but casual clothes and gorgeous accessories at fair prices, this store is also generous with sales and coupons, so don't be shy about giving out your e-mail address.

- **Great for:** Jewelry, casual tops, work dresses, and shoes
- **Online shopping available?** Yes (www.loft.com)
- **Look out for:** Their tall section. Although it's available only online, the selection is extensive and stocked with their best-selling items in longer lengths.

Old Navy. If you haven't visited this low-cost staple in a while, stop in the next time you're near one. What they have might surprise you—in addition to the reliable collection of basic tees and tanks, the store stocks inexpensive interpretations of current trends that would fool a casual observer.

- **Great for:** Activewear, casual winter essentials (e.g., fleece jackets and down vests), basics, and jeans (especially their Rockstar denim line)
- **Online shopping available?** Yes (www.oldnavy.com)
- **Look out for:** Weekend sales and online discount codes that can save you up to 30 percent

There's an App for That

Use technology to your advantage! These helpful (and free) apps can make shopping a breeze.

Snapette. Using GPS technology, this photo-sharing site can help you locate that "it" item near you! *Available for iOS and Android; free*

The Find. Ever wonder if you're getting the best deal? This app can tell you. With a quick scan of any barcode, you'll know if another store has your item for less. *Available for iOS and Android; free*

RedLaser. Similar to the Find, this app tracks down better prices based on a barcode scan. Search at stores near you (and get directions there) or online (and link directly to the site). *Available for iOS and Android; free*

Tango Card. Stop hauling around your collection of gift cards for when the shopping mood strikes—this app virtually stores and organizes all your gift cards and allows you to check balances and receive notifications if they're nearing expiration. *Available for iOS and Android; free*

Coupon Sherpa. This handy app brings hundreds of coupons from major retailers to your phone. *Available for iOS and Android; free*

Key Ring. Keep your key chain clutter-free by uploading all your loyalty-card information onto this app. When you're ready to buy, simply scan your phone and save! *Available for iOS and Android; free*

Department Stores

Hard to resist and impossible to avoid, department stores don't always have the lowest prices, but at least they raise the bar on the shopping experience, giving you some bonus bang for your buck. As with the loyalty programs we discussed in Chapter 5, high-end department stores tend to offer perks to customers as an incentive to shop there, and one of the most useful is a personal shopper. Sounds expensive, right? Wrong! The following stores all offer complimentary personal shoppers (see individual stores for a full list of related services):

- **BLOOMINGDALE'S**

- **LORD & TAYLOR**

- **MACY'S**

- **NORDSTROM**

- **SAKS FIFTH AVENUE**

- Bonus: **J.CREW** and **TOPSHOP** offer similar services as well!

Haute Hint

While many department stores skimp on coupons, Macy's is the exception, offering fantastic discounts via weekend circulars, the store's website, and e-mail—so be sure to sign up! If you forget, you can always pull up a current coupon on your smartphone and the salesperson will be able to honor the code straight from your screen.

Personal Shopping Secrets

While I personally have never taken advantage of personal shopping services at department stores—I love picking out my own clothes too much!—here are some tips for those of you who want to try them out:

1. Be honest about your budget up front. There's no sense in wasting their time or yours by being embarrassed about what you can afford to spend.

2. Be honest about what you do and don't like and what you already have. You won't hurt their feelings if you say you don't like something they've picked out—it's their job to find something you *do* love, so let them!

3. Still, be open-minded when they bring you items. Never count something out until you try it on.

4. Don't go in aimless. Give them three very specific goals to accomplish (e.g., I want to spice up my wardrobe with color; I want to add more professional pieces to my closet; and I want pieces that can transition from day to night). These are tangible and manageable goals, which will give you the best results.

5. Don't feel bad about returning anything that doesn't work for you! Sometimes you need to be in your own closet to make a permanent decision.

6. Be sure to thank them for their help and refer them to a friend if they do a great job.

Other Favorites

Spending a good deal of my time in New York as I do, I'm spoiled by the fact that just about every retailer has a storefront somewhere within the city limits. But I realize that's not the case in every town in the country. Fortunately, some of my favorite shopping sources that aren't as prevalent as an Urban Outfitters or a JCP are still shoppable no matter where you live, thanks to their inclusive online stores. Here are some of the best brick-and-mortar stores that also offer stellar web shopping:

- **MADEWELL (WWW.MADEWELL.COM)**

  Great for: shoes, rail-straight jeans, button-downs, and scarves

- **ARITZIA (WWW.ARITZIA.COM)**

  Great for: blazers and cool casual pieces like T-shirts, sweatshirts, and leggings

- **JOE FRESH (WWW.JOEFRESH.COM)**

  Great for: silk blouses and easy work separates

- **UNIQLO (WWW.UNIQLO.COM)**

  Great for: affordable cashmere sweaters and jeans

- **TOPSHOP (WWW.TOPSHOP.COM)**

  Great for: dresses, funky shoes, and jewelry

- **LOVE CULTURE (WWW.LOVECULTURE.COM)**

  Great for: superaffordable trends (think of it as a new Forever 21)

- **CALL IT SPRING (WWW.CALLITSPRING.COM)**

  Great for: colorful sandals for summer and vegan-leather handbags

- **SOUTH MOON UNDER (WWW.SOUTHMOONUNDER.COM)**

  Great for: swimsuits (look out for their sales) and jewelry from up-and-coming independent designers

OUTLETS

Beginning in the 1930s, stores began selling clothing that didn't meet company standards to employees at discounted prices, a practice that eventually spread to customers outside the company. These makeshift stores, known as factory outlets, were so called because they were often attached to the actual manufacturing factories. Eventually, freestanding outlet stores began appearing, with the earliest popping up in the eastern United States. Then, in 1974, the first outlet mall opened in Reading, Pennsylvania. In those days, the stores sold at a reduced price only imperfect garments or overruns that didn't sell from the flagship store in an effort to make some of the cost back rather than let the garments go to waste.

Today, however, the outlet business has dramatically changed. Some stores still follow the same business model as the original outlets, but more and more often, many businesses actually manufacture or buy clothes specifically to sell in their factory stores. This is not clothing that sat on a shelf at the mall; it's an entirely different product—and oftentimes, at an entirely different quality level—from what is sold in flagships. The prices are still lower than what you'd see in the full-fledged stores, but it's not because they've been deeply discounted—it's because the quality doesn't warrant a higher price.

This makes outlets not just a way for stores to rid themselves of extra inventory but a lucrative business all their own, especially in today's cash-strapped economy, in which consumers are flocking anyplace they can get a lower price.

All that said, I still think outlets are a great resource for budget-conscious Chicas. There are some truly awesome deals to be had—both at overflow outlets and at this new breed of factory stores—if you know what to look for. When you're dealing with products created specifically for a factory store, just be sure to honestly assess quality, which varies from brand to brand. Some stores' lower-price offerings are still constructed well and made from reliable fabrics—and some just plain aren't.

Haute Hint

How can you tell the difference between the two kinds of outlet stores? A few of the easiest ways:

- **Check the tag.** Tags on merchandise brought in from the full-price stores will often be struck through with a marker or sliced. Products originally manufactured for an outlet will typically say "outlet" or "factory store" on the label or otherwise be different from tags from the full-price stores. The coloring of Gap Outlet labels, (*continued*) for instance, is the reverse of that of their full-price counterparts (white labels with navy writing vs. navy labels with white writing, respectively).

- **Try asking a salesperson.** Most employees are well versed in where their goods come from and will be honest with you. Carrying merchandise made specifically for outlet stores isn't intended to be tricky; it's simply done to offer more product to the consumer—so you're not breaking the rules by bringing it up.
- **Inspect the quality.** Familiarize yourself with the detailing and construction of similar garments in full-price stores; then compare them to what's for sale at the outlet. If they seem about the same, you're likely looking at an overflow item. If the stitching, hardware, or lining is very different from what you usually see in the full-price store, the garment is likely intended for outlet.
- **Consider the season.** If something in an outlet is in season, chances are it's manufactured specifically for the factory store. True outlets usually have merchandise from a season or two prior.
- **The more stores there are, the less likely the product you find in them is true overrun.** Think about it: There's not enough merchandise at Neiman Marcus to fill hundreds of outlet stores, which is why Last Call locations (Neiman Marcus's outlet arm) are few and far between. If a store can be found at every outlet mall in the country, you can bet that you're not getting a full-quality product.

The Ins and Outs of Outlets

I asked Karen E. Fluharty—the president of New York–based Strategy Plus Style Marketing Group, who over the last twenty years has helped open nearly twenty outlet centers in the United States, Japan, Korea, and Malaysia—to share some of her industry knowledge. She explains how the business has changed and how to make outlets work for you.

Q: What led to the change in the way some outlets do business, transitioning from selling only overrun goods to manufacturing goods for their factory stores?

A: The manufacturers found that you need to be able to offer consumers full-size runs, more than just size fourteens, and you need to offer a depth of product. Each brand manages their outlet business differently, so there are stores such as Brooks Brothers Factory Store and Polo Ralph Lauren Factory Store that do manufacture for outlet, but they do this because it allows them to offer value.

Q: How does the quality compare in overrun stores and manufactured-for-outlet stores?

A: You may see different buttons or different closures or some different stitching, but whether it's made for outlet or it's overrun, the retailer will still provide a quality product because they're not willing to give their brand a lower-quality reputation.

Q: What tips do you have for outlet shoppers?

A: Shop the brands that you know and love, because you know what they cost at full price so you'll understand that the savings are there. Start shopping from the back of the store and work your way forward, because the back of the store is where all the really great deals are. And shop the sale weekends. Whether it's Labor Day, Memorial Day, Fourth of July, Presidents' Day—all of those three-day weekends are historically sale periods within the outlets, and there are even more amazing savings during those times.

We've likely all been inside a Gap Outlet at some point, with its piles of white T-shirts as far as the eye can see. And while the Gap is all well and good if you're in a basic-tank-top-buying mood, I know we all crave a little more fashion-forwardness in our lives from time to time. But brand snobs are by no means excluded from the outlet-shopping game. You might be surprised to know that some of your favorite luxury brands have outlets, too:

- **ALLSAINTS SPITALFIELDS**

- **BOTTEGA VENETA**

- **BRUNO CUCINELLI**

- **DOLCE & GABBANA**

- **LORO PIANA**

- **MARNI**

- **MAX MARA**

- **VERSACE**

- **YVES SAINT LAURENT**

Fashion Fact

Statistically speaking, according to Karen Fluharty, partner at Strategy + Style, the average outlet shopper is:

- forty-three years old.
- married.
- highly educated, with 27 percent having at least a four-year college degree.
- relatively affluent, with 74 percent owning homes and 66 percent having financial investments.

The Art of the Steal: Outlet Stores

To make sure you're getting the best deals when you outlet shop, remember the following tips:

1. Research before you shop. Know what the full-price stores are charging so that you can be aware of how much you're really saving. And never trust the "original price" on the tag—outlets raise the suggested retail price on clothes so you think you're saving more than you actually are.

2. Try on everything before you buy. This is especially important at an outlet, as sizes vary greatly since the inventory is coming from many different locations.

3. Do quality control. If you think you're buying true overflow: Can you easily identify any errors in the making of the garment? If so, are they fixable, or does the item work for you regardless? Otherwise, does the fabric feel flimsy? Is the construction poor? Is the detailing nonexistent? The same rules apply as with regular purchases; refer to the "Bargain Versus Cheap" section in Chapter 5 to decide whether or not it's a good buy.

4. The best stuff is in the back. Clearance racks—located in the rear of most stores—are where the best deals are, and where you're more likely to find the few odds and ends that actually came from the flagship as opposed to the vast displays of well-stocked items in the front (which scream "manufactured for outlet").

5. Look for coupons. Many outlet malls have coupons at their visitors' centers or printable versions on their websites, while individual stores often mail out information on sales and special discounts.

6. Consider ease of returns. Most outlet malls are located a ways outside any major cities, so whether you're visiting from out of town or you're just at the farthest reaches of your city limits, consider that you likely can't return outlet products to full-price stores. Will you be able to come back to make a return? If not, buy carefully.

Where should you go if you're in search of the best value? The following are la crème de la crème of outlet malls:

- **WOODBURY COMMON PREMIUM OUTLETS.** Boasting the largest collection of designer stores in America, this mall, located about an hour north of New York City, is a major tourist attraction.

  Location: Central Valley, New York
  Number of stores: 220
  Sample brands: Dolce & Gabbana, Yves Saint Laurent, Fendi, Gucci, Roberto Cavalli
  Website: www.premiumoutlets.com/woodburycommon

- **DESERT HILLS PREMIUM OUTLETS.** There are many designer deals to be had at this facility, located about an hour outside Los Angeles.

  Location: Cabazon, California
  Number of stores: 130
  Sample brands: Coach, Dior, Elie Tahari, Etro, Giorgio Armani, Jimmy Choo, Prada, Salvatore Ferragamo
  Website: www.premiumoutlets.com/deserthills

- **SAN MARCOS PREMIUM OUTLETS.** *The View* once named this outlet mega-plex, located about thirty minutes south of Austin, the third-best place to shop in the world, and it's got so many great stores in one place, it's hard to argue with them!

Location: San Marcos, Texas
Number of stores: 140
Sample brands: Fendi, Gucci, Michael Kors, Loro Piana
Website: www.premiumoutlets.com/sanmarcos

Fashion Fact

There are more than two hundred outlet centers in the world representing more than three hundred chains, nearly twelve thousand stores, and around 56 million square feet of leasable space.

SECONDHAND STORES

Some people get turned off by the idea of buying used clothing. Clothes can be a very personal thing, and the idea that a garment you're buying was once someone else's can be a little, well, disconcerting. But the bounty of pre-owned riches available at secondhand stores is too plentiful to be ignored! Selling "gently used" and "like new" garments, shoes, and accessories, these stores are gold mines for one-of-a-kind pieces, often at unheard-of prices. I mean, where else might you find a Christian Dior tuxedo blazer for $2.50 or a Coach bag for $7? (And yes, I've actually found both!)

Here's the catch: You have to work for your bargains. A trip to a thrift shop means flipping through clothing rack after clothing rack packed tight with merchandise of varying degrees of quality. And unlike department stores, big-box retailers, and even outlets to a degree, secondhand stores will generally have only one of each item, so if it's not in a size that works for you or it's damaged irreparably, you're out of luck.

I wish I could say I shopped at second-hand stores more often, but with my schedule as busy as it is, I have a tendency to bypass them in favor of stores that are more of a sure thing. That's the unfortunate reality of thrifting: You may visit a handful of stores one day and not find a single item that works for you. But without a doubt, you can get great deals at thrift stores if you have the time and

[

THE BOUNTY OF PRE-OWNED RICHES
AVAILABLE AT SECONDHAND STORES IS TOO
PLENTIFUL TO BE IGNORED!

]

patience to dig through the racks and keep going back regularly. The upside to all that digging is the feeling you get when you hit the jackpot and score a great deal on a rare find!

Secondhand Strategy

To help illuminate the benefits of secondhand shopping, I sought the advice of professional thrifter Victoria Franks, who founded and runs ThriftJuice.com, a site dedicated to all things thrift. She shares with us her best tips for people who aren't frequent thrifters.

Q: How can shoppers find good secondhand stores in their area?

A: Sometimes it's worth making a trek outside the city to find the best thrift stores. City folk tend to be more thrift-savvy; therefore, the selection of goods tends to be minimal. Make a trip to an affluent suburban area outside the city—the breadth of assortment is better and the prices are cheaper. If you want to stay in the city, check out your local entertainment paper for reviews on thrift stores. Local blogs are also a great way to source the best vintage stores.

Q: What's your advice for negotiating on price?

A: I negotiate when I feel that the quality isn't there or when the garment is simply overpriced for what it is. My advice is to be friendly and honest—most of the time, thrift-store owners are willing to compromise on price when it comes to issues of quality (holes, ripped seams, stains, etc.).

There are three traditional types of secondhand stores. Let's take a look at each:

1. Thrift or charity stores

These stores sell goods that have been donated to them by people like you and me. The standards for what they'll accept are typically lower than those of other types of secondhand stores, so you might have to sort through some less desirable items to find what you're looking for. But because the store keeps all the profit (unlike consignment stores), goods are typically priced lower.

2. Consignment stores

Individuals who would rather not donate their goods can sell their unwanted clothes through consignment shops, which will pay the owner a portion of the final price if and when the item sells. These stores often set a time limit for how long they'll hold on to an item—ninety days is average—and if the garment hasn't sold, the owner must retrieve it. While the prices are higher at consignment shops than at traditional thrift shops, the clothes are often of a higher quality, as well.

Dollars & Sense

While some secondhand stores will negotiate on price, don't haggle when shopping at charity stores like Goodwill or Salvation Army, where the money raised goes to a good cause. There's a difference between being frugal and being greedy!

3. Vintage

Vintage stores are privately owned operations in which the storeowner shops for clothing to sell—often from a particular time period or pertaining to a certain theme. The selection is curated and generally of a high quality, which, in turn, means prices are steeper. But the ratio of diamonds to rough is also much more in your favor!

Before you venture out, it's helpful to do a little prep work to save yourself some time and energy. Here are my best tips for getting ready to go secondhand shopping:

- **DO YOUR RESEARCH.** Not only is it a good idea to browse style sites for inspiration and a refresher on what's current, but the best thrifters study the average prices for items they're looking for so they can know if what they've found at a secondhand store is a good deal.

- **FIND THE STORES NEAR YOU.** Sites like TheThriftShopper.com and apps like the Thrift Buddy (available for iOS; free) can help you find stores in your area easily.

There's an App for That

For shopping help on the go, the Etsy and eBay apps *(both available for iOS and Android; free)* can help you see what similar items are selling for.

- **SCOUT THE AREA.** Secondhand shops are a product of what's around them, so in nicer neighborhoods, the inventory will be similarly upscale, while in trendier parts of town or areas near college campuses, the merchandise will likewise be young and hip. Decide what types of clothes you're looking for and shop in a part of town that matches your style.

- **BE IN THE MOOD.** Secondhand shopping can be a painstaking process! Wait for a day you're up to the task, or else you'll just get frustrated and overwhelmed.

- **GIVE YOURSELF ENOUGH TIME.** This kind of shopping requires patient digging, so you'll likely need an hour or more at each store to conduct a thorough search.

- **AVOID PEAK HOURS.** For the same reasons you shouldn't shop at a discount store when it's sure to be packed (crowded stores, unorganized merchandise, picked-over selection, long lines), try to avoid shopping at thrift stores on weekends.

- **LEARN THE STORE'S SCHEDULE.** Some stores run regular promotions (half-off Tuesdays, etc.), so go on sale days for even greater discounts.

- **TRAVEL LIGHT.** An oversized handbag and a heavy coat will only slow you down! Leave what you can at home or in the trunk of your car. And don't bring the kids thrift shopping either—having a little one in tow at a thrift store creates a level of stress that you just don't need!

- **BRING A BAG.** Yes, I know: I just told you to leave your handbag at home. But it's a good idea to bring a big reusable bag to carry your potential purchases in while you shop. It's easier on your hands than holding on to a bunch of hangers, and it makes navigating tight aisles easier than it would be pushing a shopping cart around.

Dollars & Sense

Make space in your closet for new purchases—and maybe even earn some money—by bringing in a bag of unwanted clothes with you when you thrift.

- **CARRY CASH.** Some stores don't accept credit cards. Plus, shopping with cash makes you more mindful of your spending so you won't get caught up and spend more than you should.

The Art of the Steal: Secondhand Stores

Because secondhand stores are so different from standard retail operations, shopping at these establishments requires an entirely different strategy from shopping at the mall. Keep these tips in mind when shopping secondhand:

Be realistic. Trying to find a specific item may prove impossible, so keep an open mind when you're hunting, and consider similar items.

Try everything on. This is especially crucial at secondhand stores, as sizing has changed over the years. Also consider that previous owners might have altered an item.

Look for labels. The best bargains to be had are on designer brands.

Inspect your finds. Be sure to check for holes, rips, missing buttons, stains, places where the garment is stretched out, and the like. (See the next section, "Passing Judgment," for more on what's fixable and what's not.) Most secondhand stores don't take returns, so you want to make sure you love something before you walk out with it.

Be a reinventor. Your tailor can make over certain secondhand finds if the length, width, or buttons aren't cutting it for you. Or think of different ways you can use something you see: That wine rack in the housewares section might make a great scarf organizer!

Don't play the waiting game. The likelihood that someone else will snag your coveted item is extremely high. If you love something, get it now.

Make friends. If you're looking for a specific type of item, ask employees to keep their eyes open and to notify you when something similar comes in.

Go back often. Secondhand stores are constantly getting new merchandise in, so shop often for your best chance to find what you're looking for.

Shop by color. If you know you love a certain shade, focus in on items in that color family. This is an easy way for first-time secondhand shoppers to start.

Wash or dry-clean everything. You don't know where these clothes have been, so be sure to clean everything you buy. If you don't feel like forking out for dry cleaning, put your purchases in the freezer for seventy-two hours, which will kill any bacteria or moth larvae.

Style Cents

Anytime you're planning to purchase a designer item secondhand, be it at a resale shop or online, make sure you're not getting stuck with a fake by validating your purchase at My Poupette, an independent online authentication service. For a fee, the experts at My Poupette can look at photos of the item in question and deliver a verdict in as soon as a day. Alternatively, if you're looking to sell an item, they can provide a certificate of authenticity, or if you think you've been a victim of fraud, they can help you take action as well. It's your one-stop authentication shop!

Passing Judgment

Since all the clothes in secondhand stores have had previous lives, chances are you'll come across pieces with damage of some sort. But a small imperfection doesn't necessarily rule something out. So which things should you take a chance on and which should you leave alone? I've got my gavel in hand and am handing down verdicts on which items you should *keep,* which are *worth a shot,* and which you should *walk away* from.

- **STAINS.** Chances are, the previous owner tried to get them out and couldn't.
  Verdict: *walk away*

- **RING AROUND THE COLLAR.** Sweat stains can often be removed by soaking the garment in a gallon of hot water with a cup of vinegar mixed in. After a few hours, wring the item and soak it in OxiClean-infused water overnight. On most garments, the yellowing will be gone.
  Verdict: *worth a shot*

- **PIT STAINS.** Try removing yellow stains by mixing one part dishwashing soap with two parts hydrogen peroxide and letting the garment soak for one hour. (Add baking soda and scrub for particularly bad stains.)
  Verdict: *worth a shot*

- **SMELLS.** Certain smells can be removed with a lot of work, but do you really want to be scrubbing and soaking someone else's stinky shirts?
  Verdict: *walk away*

- **HOLES OR RIPS.** Unless the garment works with a "broken-in" look, holes are difficult if not impossible to disguise or fix.
  Verdict: *walk away*

- **OVERWORN.** If a garment is threadbare or shoes are terribly scuffed, there's not much you can do to fix them. The only exception is soles, which can be replaced for a price.
  Verdict: *walk away*

- **BUSTED LINING.** Be sure to flip anything you're considering inside out to inspect for issues like torn lining, and so forth. A tailor can repair or replace lining, though on bigger jobs, it can cost you a pretty penny.
  Verdict: *keep*

- **FABRIC QUALITY.** Scratch leather and suede with your fingernail to see how it holds up. Does it crack or flake off? Do fur, feather, or sequin embellishments shed when rubbed against another garment? If the answers are yes . . .
  Verdict: *walk away*

- **PILLING.** Look for pill balls wherever friction is frequent: under arms, along hips (where purses rub), and the like. On knits, these

can be nearly impossible to remove. A sweater shaver can significantly help on wool, however.
Verdict: knits, *walk away*; wool, *keep*

- **BROKEN ZIPPERS.** These can be replaced by a professional.
Verdict: *keep*

- **MISSING BUTTONS.** Check the seams of the item to see if a spare
has been stitched in. If not, simply find a similar one or replace all
the buttons if you can't find a match.
Verdict: *keep*

- **TOO LONG.** A tailor can take up a hem in minutes.
Verdict: *keep*

- **TOO SHORT.** Check the hem to see how much fabric is there. If
there's not much extra, there's nothing you can do. If there's enough
fabric there to meet your length needs, a tailor can likely let it out
enough to satisfy you.
Verdict: no allowance, *walk away*; extra fabric, *keep*

- **TOO BIG.** If the cut isn't overly complicated, a tailor can likely
remove excess fabric to make it fit.
Verdict: *worth a shot*

- **TOO SMALL.** There's absolutely zilch you can do.
Verdict: *walk away*

So now that you know *how* to shop a secondhand store, *where* should you go to test out your new prowess? Here's a city-by-city guide to some of my favorite thrift stores across the country:

ARIZONA

Scottsdale

My Sister's Closet (www.mysisterscloset.com)

With multiple locations in and around the Scottsdale area and one in San Diego, this boutique carries name-brand finds in good condition. Best of all, from their website, you can browse a selection of what they have—including price, a full description, and a one- to five-star condition rating—then call the store to purchase an item and have it shipped to you.

Phoenix

Flo's on 7th (www.flocrit.org/floson7th.html)

Selling clothes, shoes, furniture, books, music, and more, this store benefits Florence Crittenton, a group dedicated to serving young, at-risk women.

Vintage by Misty (www.vintagebymisty.com)

This downtown shop features one-of-a-kind vintage pieces from around the world, including dresses, handbags, and accessories.

CALIFORNIA

Los Angeles and surrounding area

Jet Rag (825 North La Brea Avenue, Los Angeles)

Every Sunday, the parking lot of this local favorite is jam-packed with clothes—all selling for $1 apiece—and shoppers desperate to dig for deals.

Resurrection (www.resurrectionvintage.com)

All manner of vintage is available here, from timeless brands to more cutting-edge designers.

Hidden Treasures (www.facebook.com/hiddentreasurestopanga)

Perhaps the name is a nod to its out-of-the-way location, but located just beyond the hustle and bustle of L.A., Hidden Treasures is the perfect place to score some vintage goodies.

San Francisco

Out of the Closet (www.outofthecloset.org)

Run by the AIDS Healthcare Foundation, this vintage shop—with multiple locations around the city—has a little bit of everything.

Kimberley's Consignment (www.kimberleyssf.com)

One of the longest-running consignment shops in the United States, Kimberley's features contemporary clothes, handbags, and accessories.

FLORIDA

Miami

Fly Boutique (www.flyboutiquevintage.com)

Frugal fashionistas and celebs alike have been known to score used contemporary clothes and vintage garments at this local favorite, which has two locations.

Lotus House (www.lotushousethrift.org)

Proceeds from this midtown store go to the local charity of the same name, which provides help for homeless women and children.

Miami Twice (www.miamitwice.com)

For nearly thirty years, this five-thousand-square-foot store has sold the best in used contemporary garments.

GEORGIA

Atlanta

Stefan's Vintage Clothing (1160 Euclid Avenue)

In business for more than thirty-five years, this store in Little Five Points isn't the cheapest vintage store you'll come across, but with top-notch clothes dating back as far as the early twentieth century, you get what you pay for.

ILLINOIS

Chicago

Silver Moon (www.silvermoonvintage.com)

Go gaga for gowns (bridal included) at this upscale Lincoln Park shop with dresses dating back to the 1890s.

MASSACHUSETTS

Boston and surrounding area

Vintage Taste (www.vintagetasteheli.com)

This grown-up consignment shop features high-end designers like Chanel, Louis Vuitton, Hermès, and more.

Oona's (www.oonasboston.com)

Celebs like Natalie Portman have found their way to this charming Harvard Square boutique that specializes in "experienced clothing" spanning the twentieth century.

Artifaktori (www.artifaktori.blogspot.com)

This store's Davis Square location (close to Cambridge) mixes quirky vintage finds from the fifties, sixties, seventies, and eighties with owner Amy Berkowitz's personal creations. Out-of-towners can shop via their Etsy shop (www.etsy.com/shop/artifaktori).

MINNESOTA

St. Paul

Unique Thrift Stores (www.imunique.com)

You'll have to do some digging, but shoppers rave about this North End treasure trove's astonishingly low prices on mostly contemporary clothes.

NEW JERSEY

Hawthorne

Udelco Inc. (www.udelcoinc.com)

This store doesn't bother with displays, but rather has tubs filled with vintage clothes. Though the setup is a little unorthodox, there are loads of scores to be had, with many items priced below $20.

NEW YORK

New York City

Edith Machinist (www.edithmachinist.com)

Located on the Lower East Side, this store focuses on vintage shoes, handbags, and accessories and offers online shopping for out-of-state ease.

Shareen (www.shareen.com)

Gorgeous feminine dresses are the specialty at this boutique near Union Square. Though the only private area for trying on is the bathroom, feel free to get right down to it in the store, as most shoppers do (only women are allowed in).

Fox & Fawn (www.foxandfawn.blogspot.com)

This small shop in Greenpoint, Brooklyn, features vintage and gently used modern clothes.

New York City Opera Thrift Shop (www.nycopera.com/aboutus /thriftshop.aspx)

Vogue once called this two-story shop in Gramercy Park "the highest-quality thrift shop in New York." What's more, all the money made goes toward costume production for the New York City Opera.

Cure Thrift Shop (www.curethriftshop.com)

This store's founder, Liz Wolff, suffers from type 1 diabetes and therefore raises money for research via this East Village thrift shop, which also sells its goods—clothing, accessories, furniture, art, and more—online.

Guvnor's Vintage Apparel (www.guvnorsnyc.com)

This nineteen-hundred-square-foot Park Slope vintage palace offers pre-owned goods with a sense of humor.

10 Ft. Single by Stella Dallas (285 North Sixth Street, Williamsburg, Brooklyn)

Whatever you're in the market for, there's a good chance this sprawling shop in Williamsburg, Brooklyn, has it—from funky eighties tees to midcentury prom dresses. More high-end vintage items are housed in a back room.

OREGON

Portland

Little Edie's Five & Dime (www.littleediesfiveanddime.com)

Store owner Penelope Miller warmly helps customers search high and low through her funky, Grey Gardens–inspired shop. It's a great place to find that outlier to add a pop of personality to any outfit.

Rerun (www.portlandrerun.com)

Smaller spaces usually mean higher standards, and that's the case at this neighborhood store, named Best Place to Shop in an annual city poll, that carries a varied selection of items in great condition.

PENNSYLVANIA

Philadelphia

Decades Vintage (739 South Fourth Street)

Forget the nightmares from the eighties that spill out of your attic—this Queen Village boutique focuses on true vintage.

TENNESSEE

Nashville

Local Honey (www.localhoneynashville.blogspot.com)

This mostly women's boutique in the Belmont neighborhood features carefully selected vintage pieces as well as new garments made by local designers.

Southern Thrift Store (www.southernthriftstore.com)

Don't judge this book by its cover. All sorts of goodies wait inside, and with coupons available on the store's website and discounts offered on certain color tags each day, you won't score a better deal anywhere in town.

Hip Zipper (www.hipzipper.com)

A little on the hip side, as the name suggests, this store offers plenty of vintage goods from the 1950s to 1970s.

TEXAS

Austin

Feathers (www.feathersboutiquevintage.blogspot.com)

This store, located on hip South Congress, features a well-edited and clean selection of rare vintage finds.

New Bohemia (www.facebook.com/NewBohemiaATX)

You'll find loads of sixties, seventies, and eighties vintage pieces with a southern bent here; the men's side of the store (called New Brohemia) features a lot of pearl-snap shirts.

Cream Vintage (www.creamvintage.com)

This easy-to-navigate vintage shop sells music in addition to its funky clothes, and offers alterations on both in-store and out-of-store purchases.

―――――
Dallas

Dolly Python (www.dollypythonvintage.com)

This funky East Dallas shop partnered with now-defunct local favorite Ahab Bowen, meaning even more great clothes, antiques, and odds and ends for shoppers.

Factory Girl (www.factorygirlstyle.com)

This well-curated shop in the revived Deep Ellum district sells both vintage and contemporary clothes. They're all in perfect condition and impeccably styled.

WASHINGTON

Seattle

Red Light (www.redlightvintage.com)

From costumey to couture, this local favorite has it all and boasts two locations.

Fury Consignment (www.furyconsignment.com)

Looking for high-end labels? Look no further than this Madison Park shop, which has a large collection of designer brands, including plenty of Jimmy Choo shoes.

Crossroads Trading Co. (www.crossroadstrading.com)

With a focus on contemporary duds, this well-organized shop (which has two locations in Seattle and many more in other states) has designer and staff-pick racks, which help make sorting through the many offerings a little easier.

WASHINGTON, D.C.

Secondi (www.secondi.com)

Smaller than some but incredibly well organized, this store—located in the tony neighborhood of Dupont—is a great place to snag designer duds.

Annie Creamcheese (www.anniecreamcheese.com)

This expansive Georgetown store—jam-packed with vintage wares, many designer—has received "favorite D.C. vintage store" honors from readers of *Washingtonian* magazine in the past.

Current Boutique (www.currentboutique.com)

The name here is no accident—looks sold at the four locations of this local favorite are indeed up-to-date, with lots of dresses, separates, and accessories you'll want to wear. And the store is truly a boutique, styled more like your favorite retail shop than your average thrift store.

WORK
THE WEB

Who says you have to go trolling the aisles of your neighborhood thrift store to find great deals on luxury brands? These websites specialize in secondhand designer goods:

- **BIBANDTUCK.COM.** An online marketplace that makes it possible to affordably refresh your closet by trading clothes and accessories with fellow bloggers, editors, and style-savvy users . . . the best part, no money is required. All transactions are based on the site's currency of swapping instead of spending.

- **THEREALREAL.COM.** Buy authenticated, pre-owned luxury garments via limited-time-only flash sales and ongoing designer deals.

- **PORTERO.COM.** This site sells a variety of pre-owned and vintage jewelry, accessories, and handbags, but I especially love the selection of watches. The site's thorough authentication process and quality guarantee ensure that you'll end up a happy customer.

- **FASHIONPHILE.COM.** This site features an incredible selection of designer handbags and accessories. Fashionphile also has showrooms in Beverly Hills and San Francisco, where you can make appointments to see the goods in person.

- **YOOGISCLOSET.COM.** Specializing in only the finest brands of pre-owned shoes, handbags, jewelry, and accessories, this site features a no-hassle return policy and free return shipping.

There's an App for That

Here are two of my favorite apps for buying and selling secondhand:

- **ThreadFlip.** This social marketplace allows users to upload images straight from their closet of pieces they want to sell. For buyers, this means a treasure trove of thousands of new pieces every day. *Available for iOS; free*
- **PoshMark.** iPhone users can snap images of clothing and accessories and instantly post them for others to like, comment on, share on social networks, or buy. *Available for iOS; free*

- **SHOPDECADESINC.COM.** The online offspring of chic Los Angeles vintage store Decades Inc. features vintage designer clothes, shoes, bags, and accessories from all over the world.

- **EBAY.COM.** The renowned auction site offers loads of vintage fashion—just be sure to inspect each item and vet each seller since the goods are coming from individuals rather than the site itself.

Mobile Fashion

You're a lady on the go, so why shouldn't your fashion be as well? The newest way to shop is on fashion trucks, which, like their food truck predecessors, stop at various locations around town, bringing the goods to you. Here are a few of the most notable:

AUSTIN

Bootleg (www.bootlegairstream.com)
Former stylist Sarah Ellison Lewis proved the "if you build it, they will come" ethos when she gutted an Airstream trailer and began selling high-fashion, fine footwear from a park on hip South Congress Street.

BOSTON

Haberdash Vintage (www .haberdashvintage.com)

Owner Amy Lynn Chase sells funky retro finds (ranging in price from $3 to $50) from the back of a 1950s trailer.

DALLAS

The Vintage Mobile (www.thevintagemobile.com)

Owners and husband-and-wife pair Jeremy and Kelsey Turner sell everything from sixties-era dresses and cowboy boots to housewares and accessories from their cheerful green school bus.

LOS ANGELES

Le Fashion Truck (www.lefashiontruck.com)

When Stacey Steffe and Jeanine Romo met at an arts-and-crafts market—Steffe selling vintage garments, Romo selling jewelry—the pair hit it off instantly, combining their passions to start L.A.'s first mobile fashion truck, which sells clothes and accessories from little-known local designers.

J.D. Luxe (www.jdluxefashion.com)

The offerings inside this hip, youthful truck (started by hip, youthful owners Jordana Fortaleza and Tyler Kenney) make it look like Urban Outfitters on wheels.

MINNEAPOLIS

The Fashion Mobile (www.thefashionmobile.com)

Look for this Tiffany-blue truck around the Minneapolis metro area, where it sells small, hard-to-find labels. The truck is even outfitted with a dressing room.

NEW YORK

The Styleliner (www.thestyleliner.com)

Though based in New York City, this accessories-only truck makes visits up and down the East Coast, where owner/designer Joey Wolffer sells unique jewelry, handbags, and shoes from around the world and some of her own design. Check out tour dates and shop online at the shop's site.

PORTLAND

Lodekka (www.lodekka.com)

If you've ever wanted to shop for the best in vintage dresses, shoes, and accessories in a rehabbed double-decker bus, you're in luck: Erin Sutherland's Lodekka, at the corner of North Williams Avenue and Failing Street, is for you. Items are sold through the shop's Etsy store as well.

Wanderlust (www.shopwanderlustvintage.com)

Vanessa and Dan Lurie turned a $400 sixties-era trailer into a booming business, selling vintage finds ranging from $5 to $80.

SAN FRANCISCO

Top Shelf Boutique (www.topshelfstyle.com)

The vibe? Hip. The prices? Affordable. The clothes? Local (including some designs by former Fashion Institute of Design and Merchandising students). What's not to love?

The Kippy Ding Ding (www.thekippy.com)

Reasonably priced, with a feminine focus, this 1960s trailer is stocked with vintage beauties that you can also shop online. Owners Allison Norris and Amanda Linton have an eye for "all things old, gold, sparkly, and wonderful."

ONLINE

L ast but certainly not least, we come to the Internet, otherwise known as Pajama Shopping Wonderland. Yes, where there's a will—and a WiFi connection—there's a way to find just about anything you could possibly want at a price you can afford. I'm going to introduce you to several different types of money-saving sites and tell you which are my favorites and why. Then it's up to you to surf, click, and spend (wisely)!

Online-Only Stores

If you like shopping from the comfort of your own home, there are more than a few options for you online. Most brick-and-mortar stores have a web presence, and there are also plenty of retailers that operate exclusively online without maintaining any physical locations. These sites often have better deals than traditional stores, in part because of their low overhead costs, and many offer free shipping as well. Here are some of my favorite online-only cheap-chic shopping sources (and a few that have physical locations overseas):

- **LULU'S (WWW.LULUS.COM).** Shop for well-priced dresses, tops, and bottoms in a variety of flirty, casual, and dressy styles along with jewelry and accessories.

- **BAUBLEBAR (WWW.BAUBLEBAR.COM).** The site features the latest trends in jewelry at prices that you can afford to indulge in.

- **ASOS (WWW.ASOS.COM).** While this site offers everything under the sun, I particularly love it for party dresses. Shipping is free worldwide, and you can pay for two-day rush orders if you're in a hurry to get your item in time for a big event.

- **TOBI (WWW.TOBI.COM).** Find tops, dresses, jackets, and more—all with a sexy, edgy slant.

[WHERE THERE'S A WILL—AND A WIFI CONNECTION—THERE'S A WAY TO FIND JUST ABOUT ANYTHING YOU COULD POSSIBLY WANT AT A PRICE YOU CAN AFFORD.]

- **RIVER ISLAND (WWW.RIVERISLAND.COM).** While this British outfitter does have physical stores in the UK, stateside shoppers can buy from their prolific web store, which has a heavy focus on feminine, wearable clothing.

- **WAREHOUSE (WWW.WAREHOUSE.CO.UK).** This is another UK-based fashion chain that American fashionistas can enjoy, thanks to the web. It offers gorgeous, sophisticated clothes at fast-fashion prices.

- **RUCHE (WWW.SHOPRUCHE.COM).** The only giveaway that you didn't accidentally stumble onto Anthropologie's website is the considerably lower prices on the perfectly pretty, expertly curated, and impeccably styled clothes.

- **MISS SELFRIDGE (WWW.MISSSELFRIDGE.COM).** This site offers feminine looks and classic styles with a twist.

- **CHLOE LOVES CHARLIE (WWW.CHLOELOVESCHARLIE .COM).** A vast selection of practical dresses, ladylike tops, and on-trend bottoms can be found on this site at refreshingly reasonable prices.

- **VICTORIA'S SECRET (WWW.VICTORIASSECRET.COM).** OK, so this isn't online only, even here in the United States. But while most people know this retailer for its underwear, many don't know that the company's website carries an entire range of clothes (not available in stores) to wear *over* those bras and panties as well.

- **TULLE (WWW.TULLE4US.COM).** This site offers sweet and feminine clothes that you can view individually or styled in collections.

- **NASTY GAL (WWW.NASTYGAL.COM).** The offerings on this site are bold (think graphic prints and sexy cutouts) and beautiful.

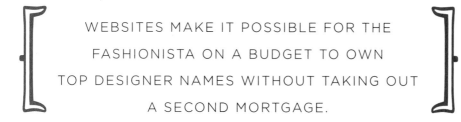

WEBSITES MAKE IT POSSIBLE FOR THE FASHIONISTA ON A BUDGET TO OWN TOP DESIGNER NAMES WITHOUT TAKING OUT A SECOND MORTGAGE.

- **PIPERLIME (WWW.PIPERLIME.COM).** Though this retailer opened its first physical store late last year, its biggest presence remains on the web, where it offers clothes and shoes in a variety of styles and prices.

- **WARBY PARKER (WWW.WARBYPARKER.COM).** Get sunglasses and prescription glasses for a steal—$95 for every pair—and for every one you purchase, a pair is donated to someone in need. A brick-and-mortar store recently opened in New York, and a mobile bus travels the country hawking the shop's wares.

Flash-Sale Sites

Flash-sale sites, online sample-sale sites, private-sale sites, invite-only shopping sites—whatever you call them, these websites make it possible for the fashionista on a budget to own top designer names without taking out a second mortgage. What a wonderful World (Wide Web)!

For the uninitiated, here's how sites like these work: They buy overstock items from sought-after designers and put their supply up for sale at a deep discount at the same time each day. These sales are accessible only to members, but entrance is a snap: Simply sign up on the site (in most cases, no payment is required, and often you're given a spending credit just for signing up).

Sales typically last a few days or less, or until items sell out, so when you see something you love, you've got to snag it fast. If you're an impulsive spender, these sites can prove dangerous, as the against-the-clock rush can encourage you to hit "buy" even before you're really sure about a purchase. My best advice is to stick to the shopping list we created in Chapter 4,

Haute Hint

If you like the rush of a flash sale but prefer it in the flesh, you need to check out sample sales, where designer clothing is sold to the public at deeply discounted prices. But do you know where and when to find them? Without the proper resources, these special events can be more elusive than a pair of flats in a Kardashian's closet.

An estimated 70 percent of sample sales take place in New York, though they're growing in other major metropolitan areas like Los Angeles. Racked.com is an excellent resource for sample sales in New York, L.A., San Francisco, Boston, and Chicago. The site's "sale listings" and "deal feeds" are updated daily with address information and pictures from the front lines.

For New York only, be sure to also check out:

- SoifferHaskin.com
- Clothingline.com
- TheStylishCity.com
- Mizhattan.com
- TopButton.com
- LazarShopping.com

For L.A., try:

- FashionDistrict.org
- CaliforniaMarketCenter.com
- ShopaholicSampleSales.com

and buy something only when an item you've been hunting for pops up at a good price.

Ready to shop? Here are my favorite flash-sale sites to check out:

- **RUE LA LA (WWW.RUELALA.COM).** In addition to designer clothing, shoes, and accessories, Rue La La offers up to 80 percent discounts on travel deals, home goods, kids' items, and more. Preview the next four days' worth of sales in the "Coming Soon" section. And as a bonus, once you pay the $9.95 shipping fee, you can ship anything for free for the next thirty days.

  App available? Yes (for iOS and Android)
  Return policy: Within thirty days of receiving your purchase, you can receive a refund on any items that are not final sale (minus a $9.95 return shipping charge) or exchange for merchandise credit in the full amount.
  Referral credit: $10
  Sales last: 48 hours

- **GILT (WWW.GILT.COM).** The mother of all sample-sale sites, Gilt introduces new sales every day—often up to a dozen at a time—on brands like Marc Jacobs, Diane von Furstenberg, and Chloe. Prices are up to 60 percent off retail, and shipping for an unlimited number of purchases is only $5.95. You can preview upcoming sales so you know when to shop.

  App available? Yes (for iOS and Android)
  Return policy: Sized items are returnable; nonsized items are not. On purchases over $200, you can get either Gilt merchandise

credit in the full amount or a refund in the original form of payment minus a $9.95 restocking fee; purchases of $199 and under can be returned for credit only.

Referral credit: $25

Sales last: 36 to 48 hours

- **HAUTELOOK (WWW.HAUTELOOK.COM).** Every morning at 11 A.M. Eastern time, HauteLook rolls out discounts (typically 50 to 75 percent off) on midrange brands like Enzo Angiolini, Elie Tahari, and American Apparel. The site features limited home and beauty offerings as well.

  App available? Yes (for iOS and Android)

  Return policy: Returns are accepted on most items for up to twenty-one days from ship date. Choose a merchandise credit for a full refund; if you opt to receive your money back in your original payment form, you lose the $5.95 shipping fee.

  Referral credit: $10

  Sales last: 48 hours

- **IDEELI (WWW.IDEELI.COM).** Shop from more than a thousand brands (ranging from diffusion lines like O by Oscar de la Renta to designers like Calvin Klein and Jessica Simpson) through ideeli's daily dozen-plus sales, which begin at 12 P.M. Eastern time. (Some bonus sales begin at 7 P.M. Eastern time.) As with Rue La La, pay for shipping once ($9.95), and get free shipping for a month. You can also review the next two days' sales, and live chatting makes customer service a breeze. Bonus: Plus sizes are available in many styles.

App available? Yes (for iOS only)

Return policy: Returns are accepted on most items for up to twenty-one days after ship date for a refund (minus a $7.95 return shipping charge) or for a full merchandise credit.

Referral credit: $25

Sales last: 24 to 48 hours

- **MYHABIT (WWW.MYHABIT.COM).** This site was founded by your favorite online retailer, Amazon.com, so it's easy to sign up using your Amazon log-in information. Score clothes, accessories, housewares, toys, books, and beauty products at up to 60 percent off starting at 12 P.M. Eastern time, and preview the next six days' events as well. Best of all, refund credit is issued in the form of Amazon.com gift cards, which you can use either on MyHabit or on anything in the vast Amazon cache.

App available? Yes (for iOS and Android)

Return policy: Eligible items may be returned for up to twenty-one days from the delivery date for a refund minus a $4.95 restocking fee, or in full for an Amazon.com gift card.

Referral credit: $25 for every five friends you refer

Sales last: 72 hours

- **BEYOND THE RACK (WWW.BEYONDTHERACK.COM).** There are crazy-good deals to be had on this site, including women's and men's fashion (brands range from Christian Louboutin to Chinese Laundry), kids' goodies, plus-size clothing, and housewares. Sales start at 9 A.M. and 5 P.M. Eastern time, though you can preview a couple of days ahead of time.

App available? No

Return policy: Returns are accepted on eligible items for credit only, minus the $9.95 shipping charge.

Referral credit: $10

Sales last: Typically 48 hours

- **MODNIQUE (WWW.MODNIQUE.COM).** Like the other sites, Modnique offers designer brands at prices between 50 and 85 percent off retail price. Unlike the other sites, however, Modnique will occasionally have some vintage offerings, or even No Reasonable Offers Refused sales events, in which you can submit a bid on an item and see if it's accepted. Sales typically start at 9 A.M. Eastern time.

   App available? Yes (for Android only) but you can access a mobile version of the site on your phone at m.modnique.com

   Return policy: Eligible items can be returned for up to thirty days from ship date. Certain items marked "store credit only" can receive only merchandise credit, which expires after one year.

   Referral credit: 10 percent of the price of the first purchase of each friend you refer

   Sales last: 36 to 72 hours

- **THEREALREAL (WWW.THEREALREAL.COM).** Buy pre-owned, authenticated goods from designers like Alexander Wang, Balenciaga, and Phillip Lim on the clock (beginning each day at 10 A.M. Eastern time), or shop from their round-the-clock contemporary designer shop. You can also consign with them if you have designer duds you're looking to get rid of. Preview sales up to a week in advance and request reminders so you never miss out on a great deal. Those who want to get a jump on other shoppers can become a First Look Member for $5 a month and get access to sales twenty-four hours before everyone else.

App available? Yes (for iOS only)
Return policy: Credit card refunds are offered on items that are not final sale within fourteen days of shipment.
Referral credit: $25
Sales last: 72 hours

- **EDITORS' CLOSET (WWW.EDITORSCLOSET.COM).** With the finest in designer clothing and accessories, this site offers free shipping on all orders and same-day shipping on any order placed before 2 P.M. Eastern time. It also guarantees authenticity on all items.

App available? No
Return policy: Returns on all but final-sale items are given store credit (minus shipping, handling, and taxes) for up to fourteen days after delivery.
Referral credit: $25
Sales last: 24 to 72 hours

- **FASHION VAULT (WWW.EBAY.COM/RPP/FASHIONVAULT).** eBay, the world's most trusted auction site, runs this flash-sale site, which features authorized independent sellers who offer designer goods at up to 80 percent off. Shipping is free and sales go on longer than on most flash-sale sites.

1

Skinny jeans

2

Leather jacket

3

Printed pant

4

White button-down

13

Black dress

5

Tweed blazer

12

Crewneck sweater

6

Leather skirt

11

Boyfriend cardigan

13

Lucky

Think you can't get a month's worth of looks from these 13 items? TURN THE PAGE TO FIND OUT HOW.>>>

7

Pencil skirt

10

Polka-dot blouse

9

Black pumps

8

Ankle boot

Colored cardigan

Striped blouse

Floral skirt

White jeans

Twill shorts

Nude peep-toe pumps

Chambray shirt

13

Lucky

Now it's time to spring forward. See how these 13 pieces turn into 30 essential Spring looks!

TURN THE PAGE TO FIND OUT HOW.>>>

Cotton dress

White T-shirt

Printed dress

Striped blazer

Flats

Colored trousers

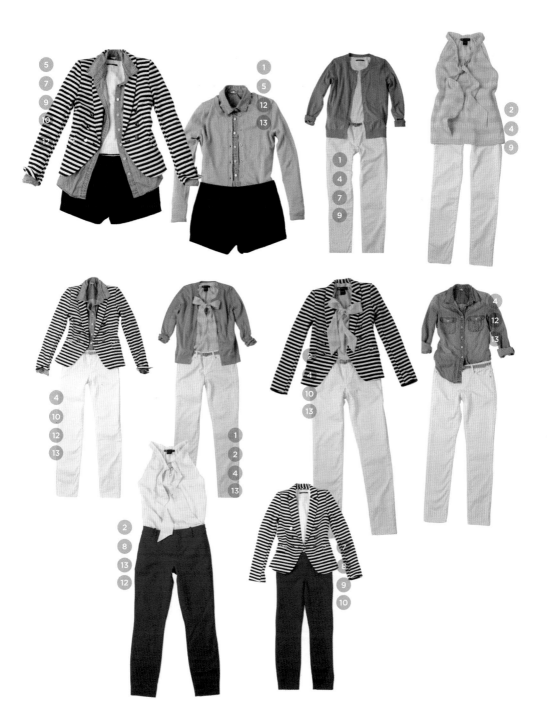

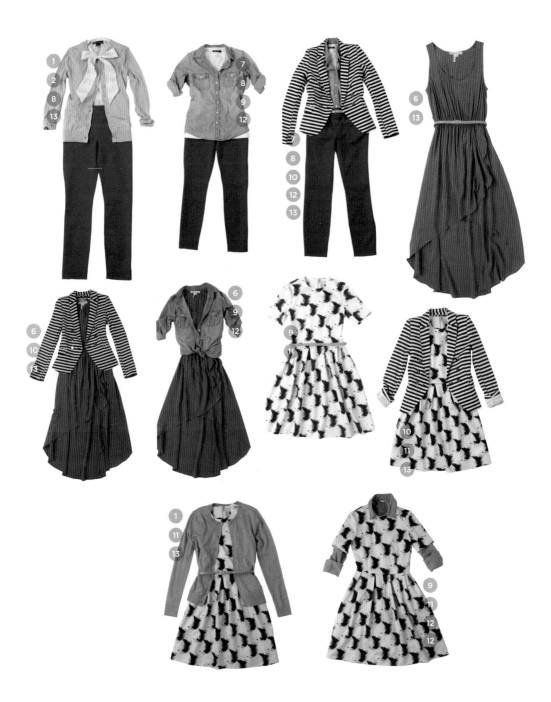

*Reinventing
the
Color
Wheel*

Yellow and Gray

Red and Purple

Fall
and
Winter

Oxblood and Rose

Cream and White

Mint and Black

Emerald and Fuchsia

Spring
and
Summer

Black and White

Army Green and Neon Pink

Three Degrees of Dressing

COOL   WARM   HAUTE

Whether you're a fashion neophyte or an outfitting expert, *turn up the heat on these five wardrobe essentials* with my cool-to-haute styling suggestions.

COOL   WARM   HAUTE

COOL　　　WARM　　　HAUTE

COOL   WARM   HAUTE

COOL   WARM   HAUTE

App available? Yes, via the eBay Fashion app

Return policy: Most items can be returned within fourteen days of receiving the item, but always check policies with each individual seller.

Referral credit: None

Sales last: Usually a week or less

- **BELLE&CLIVE(WWW.BELLEANDCLIVE.COM).** This sample-sale site is owned by Bluefly and offers both new and vintage clothing and accessories. Sales usually start at 11:30 A.M. Eastern time, though the site will throw in a spontaneous sale or two (while always letting members know about it in advance). Free standard shipping is available on all purchases.

App available? No

Return policy: Returns are accepted for up to twenty-one days from the date of purchase. Receive the full amount in-store credit, or get the total in the original form of payment minus $6.95 in return shipping.

Referral credit: $25 (and referred friends receive $10 off their first purchase). You can also like Belle & Clive on Facebook to get $20 off a purchase over $100.

Sales last: 48 to 72 hours

The Art of the Steal: Flash-Sale Sites

Here's how to get the most out of your flash-sale-site shopping experience:

1. Work from the bottom up. Most people click on the first sale and work their way down, which means that those items will sell out first. Start at the bottom to score great deals before the rest of the populace even gets to them!

2. If you need a minute to think about something or research the price, put it in your cart, which will let you hold an item for a few minutes before releasing it.

3. Get on the list. If something does sell out, don't despair—put yourself on the item's waiting list. There's a chance that the item will be returned or, if the item was popular enough, that the site will request more merchandise from the manufacturer.

4. Know the return policy. If you're unsure of something, be sure to check to see if the item is returnable. Oftentimes, unsized items like handbags and intimate items like bathing suits aren't.

5. Watch your credits. The credits you earn from referring friends often expire, so keep tabs on them so as not to let them go to waste.

Dollars & Sense

Sometimes the "retail price" listed on flash-sale sites is deceivingly high, making the sale price seem exceptionally low. When you're considering such a purchase, put the item in your cart, which allows you to hold it for several minutes, and do a quick online search for the brand in question on a site like ShopStyle.com. See what the brand typically sells for and gauge for yourself how good a deal you're really getting.

6. Mind the ship date. Some items won't ship for weeks after they're purchased, so pay close attention if you need a garment for a time-sensitive event.

7. Be sale savvy. Even flash-sale sites have sales, so keep an eye out for even further reduced prices.

8. Have a website do the work for you. Certain sites like RetailFetish .com compile deals from various sale sites so you don't have to go hunting all over the Internet.

AUCTION SITES: A WORD OF CAUTION

There are a number of auction sites out there that claim to get you great deals on new or used items—but the only online auction site I trust my money with is eBay, and their fashion component, eBay Fashion (www.ebay/fashion). Also, stay away from so-called penny-auction sites, where you purchase "bid packs" (often for 50 cents to $1 per bid) to bid on an item. These sites are more comparable to online gambling than auctions—because of the pay-to-play setup, you lose money even if you don't win the item up for grabs—and many users have reported money mismanagement or shady sales tactics. Even on eBay, you should be careful when purchasing from an individual online. Here are a few tips to help you keep from getting ripped off:

1. If you're buying something pricey, don't be afraid to ask for more photos, close-ups, pictures of the tag, and the like. You don't want to be duped into buying something only to find out that the brand, quality, or condition wasn't as advertised.

2. If you're buying a designer brand, ask for a scan or photo of the original receipt. This can help you make sure you're not purchasing a stolen good.

3. Examine the photos. Do they look like they were copied from a department store site? Do the photos seem inconsistent in lighting, backdrop, and so on, as though they might've been culled from different online listings? If so, chances are, something's fishy.

4. Check the seller's rating and read the seller's customer reviews. I don't like to purchase items from anyone with a rating below 95 percent positive.

5. The ability to return is a must. Even if their policy says returns are not accepted but you're interested in the item, try sending the seller an e-mail—some will change the auction notes to accept returns within a reasonable period of time (usually three days).

Renting

You'll recall our discussion in Chapter 5 about cost per wear—how it's not worth it to spend a lot of money on pieces that you're not going to wear very often. That very concept helped spawn an entire branch of fashion, in which customers rent rather than buy articles of clothing that would otherwise be out of their price range or are simply not something they'd likely wear again. Multiple sites have popped up that offer gowns, handbags, and accessories that can be leased for a few days for a small portion of the price of the garment.

There are pros and cons to this type of arrangement:

Pros

1. You don't have to pay big bucks for something you plan to wear only once.
2. You're doing your part to recycle by reusing someone else's clothes rather than buying something new.
3. You can have a new outfit for every occasion and in brands that you ordinarily might not be able to afford.
4. It's quick and easy, saving you precious shopping minutes.

Cons

1. You won't know for certain how the garment fits or looks until it's on, and you often can't exchange it for another size in time for your event.
2. You're still paying money, and with most sites, you don't have the option to wear it again to reduce the cost per wear.
3. There is often a dearth of sizes for plus-size and petite women.

That said, for the right occasion, this type of transaction can prove very convenient and cost-efficient. Here are a few of my favorite sites to try:

- **RENT THE RUNWAY (WWW.RENTTHERUNWAY.COM).** The most trusted name in gown rental, Rent the Runway allows you to rent designer gowns at 10 percent of the retail price. Best of all, the site always provides a second size with every order to guar-

YOU DON'T HAVE TO PAY BIG BUCKS FOR SOMETHING YOU PLAN TO WEAR ONLY ONCE.

antee a good fit. Reserve your dress up to six months in advance and choose from either a four-day or eight-day rental period, depending on your needs. Another bonus: If you don't like the dress when it arrives, or it doesn't fit, you can exchange it for another.

Rents: Gowns, jewelry, and handbags
Shipping: $9.95 standard; expedited options for a higher fee (same-day service available in New York); return shipping is free
Insurance: Included in the cost of the garment; if the item is damaged beyond repair, your credit card will be charged the full retail price
Late fees: 5 percent of the retail price per day

• **LENDING LUXURY (WWW.LENDINGLUXURY.COM).** In addition to renting out tops and bottoms as well as dresses, this site allows you to purchase a garment. (The more times something's been rented, the lower the asking price.) The downside? You're sent only one size per order, and you can exchange for a different size only on your first rental of a specific designer.

Rents: Dresses (long and short), tops, and bottoms
Shipping: Several shipping options, depending on how fast you need your item; cost is determined based on your location; return shipping is free
Insurance: Each garment comes with a free insurance policy worth up to $100. If repair costs go beyond $100, you will be charged for the remainder.
Late fees: $15 per day for the first two days; after that, you're charged the rental fee again

- **LE TOTE (WWW.LETOTE.COM).** Much like Netflix does for movies, Le Tote allows you to borrow an unlimited number of clothing items for $49 per month. Fill out a style profile and the site's stylists will put together outfits for you, then send you three garments and two accessories at a time, in a darling tote bag. Keep them as long as you like and then send them back to get your next tote full of goodies (or buy them at retail price if you like)!

  Rents: Dresses, tops, and accessories
  Shipping: Free both ways
  Insurance: $5 charge for minor repairs; if an item is lost, stolen, or damaged beyond repair, you're charged the retail price of the item
  Late fees: None—as long as your monthly subscription fees are paid, you can keep your items as long as you want

- **BAG BORROW OR STEAL (WWW.BAGBORROWORSTEAL .COM).** Chanel, Chloe, Louis Vuitton . . . this site has them all! Rental periods are longer than with most rental sites—choose from one-week, one-month, or three-month options—but you can keep the item even longer if you like (you'll just be charged again at the end of the rental period). Unlike the gown sites, this one offers full refunds (less shipping) in the original form of payment if you're unsatisfied with your order. Sadly, you're not able to purchase your bag—unless it's going to BBOS Private Sale.

  Rents: Handbags, clutches, jewelry, and sunglasses
  Shipping: Free standard shipping both ways; expedited shipping is available for a fee
  Insurance: Included in the rental cost; if the item is lost or stolen, you'll be charged the full retail price

Late fees: None; you'll just be charged the rental fee again at the end of the borrowing period

- **BORROWED BLING (WWW.BORROWEDBLING.COM).** In order to rent from this site, you've got to sign up for one of three tiers of monthly plans, which, depending on the level, allow you to have two or three pieces out at a time (which you can keep for as long as you want, provided your dues are paid). Beyond the monthly fee, however, there is no rental cost. Both members and nonmembers can purchase from the site.

Rents: Earrings, necklaces, bracelets, rings, watches, broaches, evening bags, and sunglasses

Shipping: $9.99 round-trip shipping

Insurance: None; you will be charged the cost of any repairs to fix damage beyond typical wear and tear

Late fees: None, as long as your monthly membership dues are paid

- **ADORN BRIDES (WWW.ADORN.COM).** When your big day rolls around, take care of the something borrowed with one click! Choose from this site's curated selection of diamond and pearl jewels in classic styles (some, like the Middleton earrings, are celebrity inspired). Rental fees can be as little as 2 percent of the price of the item, but items cannot be purchased.

Work the Web

To make shopping online easier, keep a spreadsheet of your measurements and sizes in different brands on your phone or in a Dropbox folder so you can access it wherever you are. Update it every time you shop so it's always up-to-date. It just takes a second to do but will save you tons of time—and the hassle of returning something that doesn't fit!

Rents: Earrings, necklaces, bracelets, hair accessories, and clutches
Shipping: Free shipping on orders of $300 or more; free return shipping
Insurance: Included in the rental price
Late fees: 20 percent of the rental fee on the first day, 100 percent of the rental fee for two to seven days, 200 percent of the rental fee on days eight through fourteen; after two weeks, you may be charged the full retail price

• • •

There you have it: every single one of my best-kept secrets for looking fab for next to nothing. I hope I've been able to shed some light on ways to shop chicly yet cheaply that will work within your budget and lifestyle.

As I've said before, a low price alone doesn't make something a good buy. A steal is a steal only if it's also something you love and something that enhances what you already own to help convey who you are to the world. Don't forget that your style is a reflection of you—both who you are as a whole and how you feel that particular day—so don't settle for clothes that make you feel anything but spectacular, or like anyone but yourself.

[DON'T SETTLE FOR CLOTHES THAT MAKE YOU FEEL ANYTHING BUT SPECTACULAR, OR LIKE ANYONE BUT YOURSELF.]

It's important to remember that style isn't finite; it isn't something you achieve and then have forever. Rather, it's a journey—an ongoing quest for self-expression and a lifelong search for the pieces that accomplish that. And just as style is a very conscious, mindful process, the way you shop for it should be as well. Using the resources I've given you in this chapter, make an effort to minimize your spending while maximizing your style. That mix of ingenuity and creativity is the mark of a true artist!

STYLE ISN'T FINITE; IT ISN'T SOMETHING
YOU ACHIEVE AND THEN HAVE FOREVER.
RATHER, IT'S A JOURNEY.

THE DEVIL IS IN THE DETAILS

Chapter 7

By this point, you should feel like you've got a good grasp on how to put together a fabulous wardrobe that expresses who you are. The final step is learning how to actually style it. As with most things, the key to looking your absolute best is in the details—those little intangibles that take an outfit from so-so to so stunning. Can you create an outfit without knowing some of these tricks and tidbits? Sure. But that's the equivalent of having cake without icing on top—a little flavorless, and leaving a lot to be desired.

In this chapter, I'll tackle those little odds and ends that most people either overlook or are simply unsure about. I'll address common fashion questions and conundrums and give you primers on fit, color, and mixing and matching. I'll give you practical how-tos, dos and don'ts, and lists of must-haves. In the end, you'll be armed with all the expert advice you need to make memorable, show-stopping ensembles.

FIT

Perhaps the most important detail when dressing is fit. How clothes hang on your frame and hug your curves can make all the difference in how an outfit looks. If something is too big, small, long, short, or baggy, you run the risk of looking heavier, shorter, or—OK, I'll say it—skankier than you really are. You could even hurt yourself! (Improperly fitting shoes can do real damage to your feet.)

Adhere to the following fit guides for each item in your closet. If something doesn't fit like it should, bring it to your tailor to make alterations where possible. If it's not fixable, toss it!

Shoes

Shoes should fit the length of your foot snugly, without squishing your toes. If you can fit a finger between the back of your heel and the back of the shoe, the shoe is too large. Pay attention to width as well; if you have too

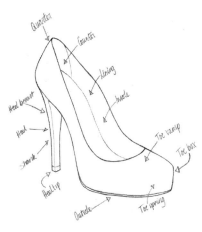

much or too little give on the sides, ask the clerk if narrow or wide sizes are available. The severity of your arch can greatly impact fit too. A low arch can put undue pressure on certain parts of your feet, as can an abnormally high arch.

Keep in mind that the shape and style of the shoe will affect how

Haute Hint

Shoe sizing varies based on where the shoes were manufactured. Here's a handy conversion chart of U.S., European, and UK sizes:

U.S.	EUROPEAN	UK
5	35–36	3
5.5	36	3.5
6	36–37	4
6.5	37	4.5
7	37–38	5
7.5	38	5.5
8	38–39	6
8.5	39	6.5
9	39–40	7
9.5	40	7.5
10	40–41	8
10.5	41	8.5

it looks on your leg. A low vamp provides a leg-lengthening effect, whereas an ankle strap can visually cut the leg line, making you appear stumpier. Consider what you plan to wear the shoe with when you're trying it on.

Pants

For dress pants, the most universally flattering rise is a midrise: one that rests below the navel but above the hip. As for cut, there are an overwhelming number of options out there, including wide-leg, boot-cut, flare, straight-leg, pencil, skinny, and cropped, to name a few. Different shapes flatter different body types, but a good universal cut is one that hugs the hips and then falls straight to the floor, offering a little legroom without creating an overly baggy look.

Where you don't have a choice is in the fit of the waist and hips. They should be tailored but not tight—no bulges or pulling. If the cut is too generous in either place, a seamstress can remove some of the extra fabric. If the cut is too stingy, there's nothing a tailor can do. Also nonnegotiable is the fit in the crotch: too tight and you risk showing off more than you intended to; too loose and you look like you're wearing a diaper underneath. Like Goldilocks, you want a pair that's just right.

Jeans

Denim rises have changed dramatically over the years, but opt for a medium or conservative low rise for a flattering look that won't veer too close to momdom and will still keep your underwear concealed (as it always should be!). As far as cut is concerned, it's hard to go wrong with a simple boot cut—the jeans should be fitted through the knee and get looser toward the ankle. But as I've told you before, skinny is the new classic when it comes to denim. If you've been skittish about trying this body-conscious cut before, believe me when I tell you that these jeans can flatter *any* figure! Really! Just look for a dark wash (universally slimming and a cinch to dress up) with a bit of stretch to keep them snug. No matter which cut you prefer, stay away from whiskering, fading, distressing, and

A new technology promises to take the guesswork out of finding the right fit. Called Me-Ality, this machine—available at select malls across the nation, with more being added—scans your body with harmless radio waves, analyzes your body shape, and gives you a list of items available in the mall that will be an ideal fit!

ornate embroidery and embellishments, which detract from a timeless, clean look and draw attention to the wrong places. Pocket size and placement should be determined by the size of your derriere. Women with ample bottoms should stick to medium-sized pockets set a little higher on the butt to give the appearance of a perky rear. Ladies with less junk in the trunk can plump up their backsides with a little high-contrast stitching. Make sure you can comfortably slip at least one finger into the waistline of your pants to avoid the dreaded muffin top.

LENGTH GUIDE

Full-length skinny jeans or pants should hit right below the ankle. This ensures that they're long enough to tuck into boots, yet not so long that they puddle at the ankles when worn with heels or flats.

Ankle-length jeans or pants should come to the ankle or even an inch above (not the top of your shoe). Ankle-length bottoms in a skinny cut are more versatile than full-length pants, in my opinion, and look better with flats and ankle boots than longer cuts.

A cropped jean or pant should hit at the spot where your calf muscle tapers off. Any higher, and you're not showing off the slimmest part of your leg. Any lower and it will make your legs look awkward and stumpy.

Wide-leg or boot-cut jeans or pants should completely cover the shoe and almost graze the floor.

Style Cents

When it comes to skinny cuts, there's no need to have pairs in different lengths for wearing with heels and with flats. The beauty of this style is that they can easily switch back and forth. But to avoid too much puddling at the ankles when you wear longer pairs with flats, simply tuck the ends of the legs under. Now you get two pairs in one!

Haute Hint

Sizing for premium denim is done by size of the waistline in inches. Here's a handy conversion chart so you know which size to grab when you're trying on:

U.S. size:	0	2	4	6	8	10	12	14
Waist size:	24	25/26	26/27	28	28/29	30	32	33/34
European size:	34	36	38	40	42	44	46	48

Straight-leg jeans or pants should be hemmed (or rolled) at or just above the anklebone.

Skirts

No matter the shape, skirts should fit comfortably at the waist without gaping, or else they'll twist when you walk. If a skirt is too narrow across the hips, it will not only pull unattractively, but also inch up as you move. To test the size, sit down wearing the skirt. When you stand up, if it remains bunched up around the hips, it's too small. Hemlines should be the same distance from the ground all the way around; if a large bottom or tummy causes the length to be shorter in the front or back, have a tailor bring up the length on the opposite side.

LENGTH GUIDE

Miniskirts should hit the middle of your palm when your arms are down by your sides. *Great for:* petites.

Midiskirts should hit the bottom of your calf, or the skinniest part of your leg. *Great for:* tall ladies

Maxiskirts should graze the ground. *Great for:* all heights, even petites (Contrary to what you might think, floor lengths actually make you look taller!)

Pencil skirts should hit right below the knee and taper. Just make sure there's a vent in the back so you can walk comfortably. *Great for:* all heights and curvy girls

Knee-length skirts should graze the top of the knee. *Great for:* all heights and body types

Dresses

Refer to skirt rules for proper fit and length. Choose a cut that is flattering to your figure: an A-line flare camouflages wide hips and bottoms and a vertically color-blocked dress can make you look three sizes smaller. If your waist is small, show it off with a style that cuts in at your midsection, or belt drapey dresses to draw attention to your tiny tummy. When sporting an empire waist, be sure it hits immediately below the bust line—it should not cut off your bust.

Shirts

With button-down shirts, make sure the buttons across the largest part of your chest lay flat. If they're pulling when buttoned, you need to go a size larger. Ditto for the sweep (the bottom part of the shirt that goes around your hips)—it should comfortably fit the widest portion of your hips. Long sleeves should hit just below the wristbone. If your arms are short, get sleeves taken up so they don't puddle; if your arms are extralong, you may need to get shirts custom-made or roll up sleeves to disguise the length. As with jackets, shoulders should hit exactly at the outer curved edge of the shoulder. Don't allow for any excess bagginess in the bust or armpits. The back should lay smooth without showing any bumps or rolls—go up a size to accommodate if need be, or wear slimming undergarments. Make sure your bra size is right as well (see page 288); a poorly fitting bra can lead to unattractive bulges under shirts.

Jackets and Blazers

The shoulder seam should sit at the outer edge of your shoulders—not too far in and not sagging onto your upper arm. The armhole should not be so wide that it looks droopy in the underarm but not so tight that it will chafe. Make sure the give across the back is generous enough that you can move, stretch, and reach comfortably in without pulling at the fabric. On the other hand, a jacket with too much width will make you appear boxy or heavy. I tend to leave my blazers open, so make sure blazers are tailored enough that they look good unbuttoned.

The stance—where the lapel and buttons meet—and jacket length should be flattering to your individual shape. Petite women tend to look best in higher stances, while taller women can pull off a deeper V. Lengths vary by incoming and outgoing styles, but a classic cut hits right at the hip, though this can and should be adjusted slightly higher or lower, depending on your shape. Full-length sleeves should hit at the wristbone. Cropped sleeves should hit at the middle of the forearm and are particularly good for petite women.

Lapels and pockets should be inversely proportionate to one's bust size: Small-chested women can add bulk with larger lapels and bust-height pockets, while large-breasted women should choose thinner lapels and waist-height pockets.

Coats

Many of the same principles for jackets apply here in terms of fit. The bulkier materials used on heavy coats make for a thicker silhouette, so tailoring is especially crucial. But don't try to combat boxiness by buying a coat that's too tight—and don't forget that you'll probably be wearing sweaters underneath whatever you buy, so allow for plenty of room. Consider going up a size for true winter coats; transitional outerwear should be bought true to size. Think about length and proportions as you look, too: Longer cuts offer more warmth but can drag down a silhouette when paired with long trousers.

Bras

The majority of the support should come from the band, not the straps, as most people incorrectly believe. Therefore, it's important that the band fit snugly but not so tight that it rides up or pinches the skin on your back. The straps of your bra shouldn't slip off your shoulders or cut into them. The cups should fit against your chest without gaping open or cutting into your breasts. The panel between the cups should lay flat against your breastbone.

To determine your proper bra size:

1. Put a tape measure at band level on your back, and then bring the tape around to the front. If the measurement is an odd number, round it down to the nearest even number. This is your band size.

2. Measure around the fullest part of your chest, rounding up to the nearest whole number if your measurement ends in a half inch or more.

3. Subtract the band size from the bust size. The difference will determine your cup size:

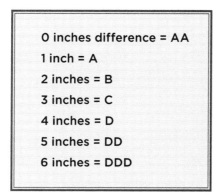

0 inches difference = AA
1 inch = A
2 inches = B
3 inches = C
4 inches = D
5 inches = DD
6 inches = DDD

MUST-HAVES
LISTS

For the most part, style is a very personal thing, tailored to the individual. But there are a few key pieces that every woman should have in her wardrobe without exception—go-to pieces that will get you through any occasion. Whether your style is a risk taker or more of a hippie chic, there will likely come a time when you need each of the following must-haves:

Five Must-Have Shoes

It's been said that the shoes make the outfit, so make yours a good one with these butt-kicking shoes:

1. Nude pumps

These go with everything and can be worn for just about any occasion: dressing up a plain dress for a hot date, heading to a job interview, or wowing at a wedding.

2. Dressy metallic high-heel sandals

While you might not get daily, or even weekly, wear out of these, when a formal event comes along, you won't want to be caught without a proper pair of party shoes.

3. High-heel black knee boots

These are a necessity in wintertime; they lend warmth and sexiness to any outfit. Wear them with jeans tucked into them, paired with a skirt, or layered over leggings.

4. Flat riding boots

These are practical for a number of occasions and comfortable to boot (pun intended).

5. Casual flats or flat sandals

Depending on the season, you need a staple shoe in a neutral color that can be worn with just about everything in your closet.

Five Must-Have Bags

Carry your stuff in style with these functional bags:

1. Weekender/overnight bag

A suitcase is overkill when you're going to be gone only a night or two. Instead, invest in a utilitarian weekender bag that stores what you need and nothing you don't.

2. Clutch

Don't sling your overstuffed satchel over your shoulder for a night on the town or a formal occasion. A delicate clutch—big enough for your ID, some cash, your phone, and your compact—lends a polished look.

3. Tote

Whether you're running errands or schlepping documents to the office, it helps to have a classic carryall to throw your things in.

4. Cross-body

This is a great choice for concerts, going shopping, or anytime you prefer to be hands-free.

5. Top-handle satchel

Sophisticated and practical, this makes a great everyday bag.

Ten Must-Have Undergarments

No, most people won't ever see them, but undergarments provide the foundation for your clothes and can make you look skinnier, firmer, and bustier without lifting a finger (or visiting a plastic surgeon). So show these hardworking pieces some love and invest in these must-haves:

1. Thongs

Look for a low rise with a wide waistband for the most comfort.

2. Seamless panties

If you can't bear to wear a thong, opt for seamless panties to avoid ending up with a visible panty line. Commando makes my favorite.

3. T-shirt bra

This full-coverage bra looks smooth under the thinnest of T-shirts.

4. Convertible bra
Reconfigurable straps allow this bra to work with a variety of shapes, including strapless, one-shoulder, racer-back, and more.

5. Push-up bra
Those of us who weren't blessed with natural fullness are forced to just fake it 'til we make it! Even if you're endowed, everyone can use a little lift.

6. Shapewear
Whether it's for your thighs, belly, bottom, or back bulge, the right shapewear can smooth out any problem areas. Spanx makes excellent, seamless versions of all types, but there are plenty of less expensive varieties.

7. Nude or black bandeau top
These undergarments help maintain modesty when worn under draped blouses or low-cut tops.

8. Half-slip
Cheap dresses and skirts tend to lack lining, so throw a half-slip on underneath to prevent sheerness or an embarrassing wind mishap.

9. Nude camisole
Slip one on under a sheer top to prevent showing off too much of your assets. Those without lace are most functional.

10. Lingerie
Don't be shy! Every woman should have something that makes her blush and her partner excited!

FAST FASHION FIXES

Sometimes a fashion emergency arises when you least expect it, and you need a temporary fix until you can address the problem more permanently. Here are some common wardrobe malfunctions and short-term solutions for each:

Problem: Your outfit is wrinkled and you don't have an iron or time to take it to the cleaners.

Solution: Use your hair flat iron.

Problem: Your dress is too long with your shorter shoes or your hem comes loose.

Solution: In lieu of a needle and thread, use double-sided tape to make a temporary hem. If you have access to an iron, press the new hemline to create a crease.

Problem: Static cling is causing your skirt to stick unattractively to your backside.

Solution: Hair spray will release the cling.

Problem: After playing with a dog, your outfit is covered in hair.

Solution: Find anything adhesive—packing tape or the backing of a FedEx mailing pouch—and press it to your garment to remove lint or hair.

Problem: You've got a loose button.

Solution: Take a twist tie from a loaf of bread and peel the paper off to reveal just the wire. Thread it through the buttonholes and twist to fasten.

Problem: The zipper on your jeans broke.

Solution: Cut a Velcro strip down to size and use that to close your fly.

Problem: You lost the ankle strap on your shoe or a fabric belt on a skirt or dress.

Solution: Replace it with a pretty ribbon for an instant update.

Problem: The rubber strap of your flip-flop pulls through the hole in the sole.

Solution: Feed the strap through the sole and attach a plastic closure tab from a bag of bread to the underside to keep it from slipping back through.

Style Cents

Want to know the secret to a $20 boob job? Pick up a pair of the silicon bra inserts commonly referred to as "chicken cutlets" or the stick-on variety and wear them in your bra. Instantly you'll get extra fullness and lift without anyone being the wiser.

BREAKING
THE RULES

Everywhere you look, there are rules. No U-turns. No personal calls at work. No running near the pool. And somewhere along the way, we learn a number of "rules" for how to dress that simply don't make sense in this day and age—and some that *never* did! Fortunately, fashion is about breaking the rules. With that in mind, here are some commonly heard fashion **"don'ts"** that are actually **"dos"**:

1. Don't wear white after Labor Day/before Easter.
You work just as hard after Labor Day as you do before, so why shouldn't your clothes be able to work it, as well? The key to wearing winter white is to look for fabrics with heft and weight in richer tones like ivory and cream.

2. Don't match your makeup to your outfit.
While being overly matchy-matchy with any part of your outfit is a beginner's move, subtly coordinating, say, your eye shadow to your top can enhance a look. Just don't overdo it—less is more in this case.

3. Don't have mismatched accessories.
Whoever said your handbag had to match your shoes obviously didn't like having any fun. Feel free to mix up tones, both within the same color family and outside it!

4. Don't wear bright colors or pastels in the winter.

Why does your wardrobe have to be lacking in color just because the foliage outside is? Fashion authorities have done away with the dull, muted palettes that were traditionally worn in winter in favor of a rainbow-ranging selection of shades. For suggestions on fun and innovative color options for each season, turn to pages 131–134.

5. Don't wear print from head to toe.

Think you can't be decked out in polka dots or top-to-bottom plaid? Talk to the industry's leading fashion houses, many of which have sent coordinated and clashing patterns down the runway in recent years. The most wearable way to do it is to mix scales of patterns and find one unifying color to tie both patterns together.

6. Don't mix different styles.

There's absolutely no reason why you shouldn't combine more than one style in the same outfit if they complement each other. A sporty jacket with a flirty skirt looks edgy and purposeful. For suggestions on easy-to-mix styles, turn to pages 314–316.

7. Don't wear lace, brocade, or sparkles for the daytime.

Glamour shouldn't be reserved for after dark. When paired with a grounding piece like dark-wash skinny jeans, your most fabulous lace top can easily do double duty. Got a sequin skirt? Wear it with a simple black tee to make the look more casual.

8. Don't wear a skirt or dress without pantyhose.

Though the Duchess of Cambridge might disagree, bare legs are A-OK when temperatures don't require a little thermal protection. If you work in a conservative office, just make sure the hem of your skirt is modest enough not to cause waves.

9. Don't mix black and blue.

Despite their association with bruising, we're not sure why such friendly colors got such a bad rap. The truth is, these two colors get along famously—provided the colors are far enough apart on the spectrum that it doesn't look like you got dressed in the dark. Introduce a third color to help make the distinction.

10. Don't mix black and brown.

For too long, two of our most popular shades have been kept at odds. No longer: Fashion fiends have embraced the interplay these two neutrals can have. For the less daring, opt for softer shades of brown to start.

11. Don't wear pink if you're a redhead.

Who says blondes and brunettes get to have all the fun? Pink is a fresh and versatile color that should be enjoyed by everyone. As is the case with most colors, though, find the shade of pink that looks best with your coloring. Those with strawberry-blond tresses should stick to pale and salmon shades, while darker, truer redheads should opt for fuchsias and berry tones.

12. Don't wear two different shades of the same color.

I absolutely love the way a sky-blue top looks with a navy skirt. Blend different tones of the same shade for a rich, polished finish.

Color Confidential

Forget the "rules" on color—I say, if you like a color, wear it! The key is finding the right *tone* that works for your individual coloring. In general, for instance, women with light or dark hair and those with pale complexions look good in saturated hues, like kelly greens, cherry reds, and royal blues, while ladies with medium skin and hair work well with more muted tones, such as forest green, lavender, and aqua. But over the course of my career working with all different types of women, I've found four shades that work with every skin tone, hair color, and eye tint.

Red: Strike the balance between a cool, cherry red and a warm, orangey shade.

Soft coral: Opt for a shade somewhere between a light pink and a peach so the effect is more of a neutral than a girly pastel.

Cobalt: It wasn't one of the colors of the year for nothing! Try this hue if you're feeling dramatic. Don't be scared to pair it with another bright for an extrabold effect.

Jade: Richer than teal but not quite as deep or serious as emerald, this color looks beautiful with gold tones and will instantly liven up any outfit.

For even more tips on fun and innovative color suggestions by season, turn to pages 131–134.

13. Don't mix metals.

If you're talking about hard-rock songs, it probably is advisable to play one tune at a time. As far as fashion is concerned, though, you're free to pair silvers and golds with reckless abandon. The easiest way to do this is with an "arm party" of different shades of bangles; then add on from there. (See page 308 for more on this.)

14. Don't mix bright colors.

You can pair loud hues without having to break out the sunglasses—if you do it carefully. Stick to two shades at a time in a simple color-blocked pattern and you'll look fashion-forward rather than fluorescent.

The Keys to Color Blocking

With so many colors in the rainbow, how can you make sure you don't go wrong when it comes to mixing hues in an outfit? Take a lesson from your elementary school art teacher for the best pairings:

Analogous colors—colors that are next to each other on the color wheel. When color-blocking with side-by-side tones, choose one to be the dominant color and merely accent with the second shade.

Examples: blue and green; red and orange

Complementary colors—colors that are on opposite sides of the color wheel. For best results, use the same saturation of each shade (brights with brights, muted with muted, etc.).

Examples: red and green; blue and orange

Triad—the three colors that appear along the points when you draw a triangle on the color wheel. No matter how you draw it, the three resulting shades will play well with one another.

Examples: red, blue, and yellow; orange, purple, and green

If you're feeling daring, here are some advanced pairings to try:

Colors that form ninety-degree angles

Examples: Blue and yellow-green; red and orange-yellow

Colors that form an X

Examples: Purple, yellow, blue, and orange; yellow-green, pink, blue-green, and red-orange

STYLIST SECRETS

One of my favorite parts of my job is getting to style real women of all shapes and sizes for TV. It's such a rewarding experience because I get to see a transformation in these women—they leave with more confidence, a brand-new outfit, and an arsenal of my best fashion tips and tricks. While every woman would love to have a personal stylist primping them before they head out the door, I know it's not realistic. Instead, I'm going to give you five of my go-to tricks that I use on almost every one of my models to empower you to be your own stylist. Next time you're putting on an outfit, try these tips:

1. Scrunch it!

Whenever there's anything long-sleeve involved, I always push up the sleeves. This goes for sweaters, button-down long-sleeve shirts, blazers, and so on. It may sound a little eighties, but showing off your forearms helps you look skinnier—and it's an easy way to look like you've been styled by a pro!

2. Belt it!

Not only do belts help create a waist (whether you have one or not) but they also help add visual interest and detail to any outfit. Try belting your blazers, cardigans, dresses—you really can't go wrong if you opt for a one- to one-and-a-half-inch version. Just remember to place the belt at your natural waist (more on that next) rather than slung low around your hips. If your item comes with a belt that matches or coordinates, don't use it. Instead, choose a belt in a contrasting color or a print like leopard to add an unexpected element to your outfit.

3. Rediscover your waist!

Do me a favor, ladies: Find the skinniest part of your midsection. This, believe it or not, is your natural waist. Not above that, not below it. If you wear your skirt lower than your waist (say on your hips), you're at risk of throwing off your proportions and looking ten pounds heavier than you really are. When it comes to skirts, I always end up moving them up on my models to accentuate their thinnest spot. Humor me, and next time you wear a skirt try this trick—you'll look slimmer in an instant!

4. Make a statement—with a necklace!

Whenever you look in the mirror and think, *Something's missing,* chances are, adding an oversized necklace will fix it! These big baubles have become my signature, and whether you're petite or plus-size, they look good on everyone. Invest in a few bold ones or layer smaller necklaces that you already own to create the same effect.

5. Tuck it in!

One of the most common mistakes I see women make is not tucking in shirts that should be tucked. I'm not saying *everything* needs to be tucked in, but you should at least try it to see how it looks before ruling it out. Tucking a shirt into a pencil skirt, for example, can help give you that tiny waist you never knew you had!

ACCESSORIES 101

Accessories can be your best friend when it comes to enhancing a look—they can add dimension and visual interest to a boring outfit, or call attention to a body part that would otherwise get ignored. And sometimes, they simply lend the extra touch of sparkle that we all crave once in a while.

Below are some quick primers on a few things that trip most people up when it comes to accessorizing. But remember: This is just my take. You can—and should—experiment with your own looks until you find your signature style!

How to. . .Tie a Scarf Six Ways

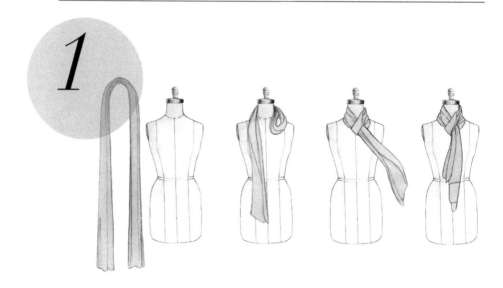

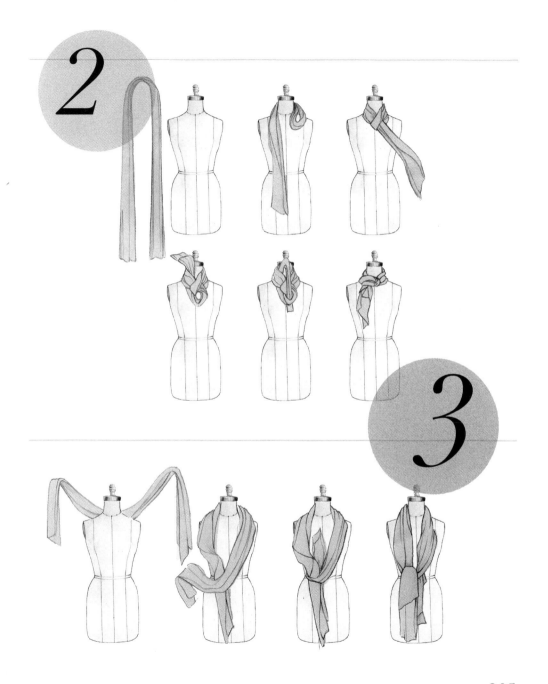

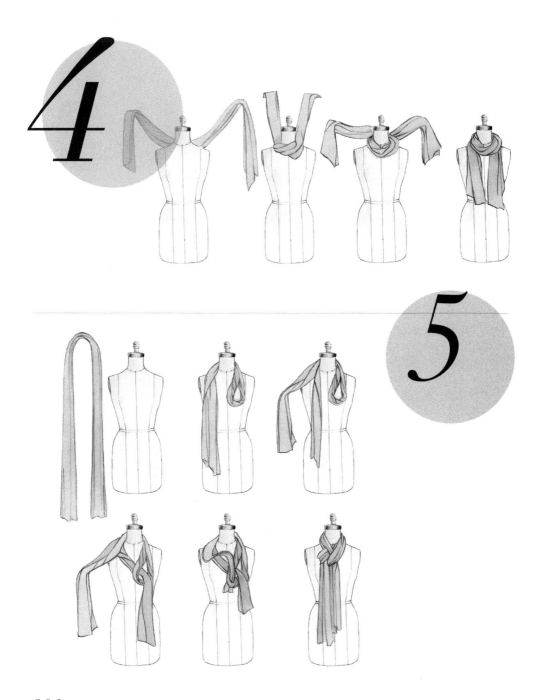

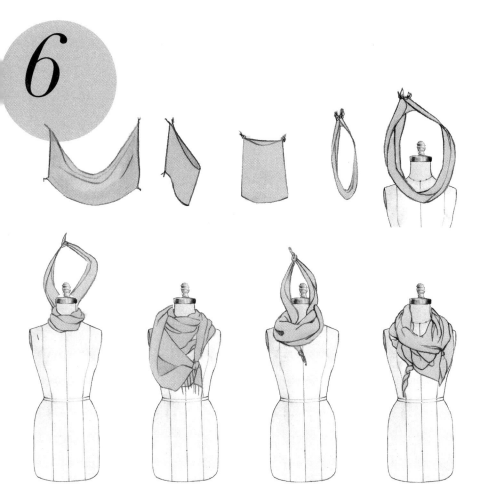

How to . . . Throw the Perfect Arm Party

One of the biggest accessories trends of late is the "arm party" look—stacking bracelets, bangles, and watches with reckless abandon. I love this "more is more" approach, especially because there's no wrong way to do it. But if you're not sure where to start, here are a few pointers:

- **DON'T BE AFRAID TO MIX METALS.** Silver and gold play nicely together when there's this much variety.

- **VARY THE BRACELET THICKNESSES,** always making sure to put the biggest ones on the bottom (meaning they go on first).

- **IT'S NOT ALL FORM OVER FUNCTION**—add a watch to the mix, too.

- **DIFFERENT TEXTURES LOOK GREAT TOGETHER,** too, but it works best if there's a common thread tying them all together. So if you've got a pebbled leather bracelet, a watch, and a cuff in the mix, maybe make sure they've all got gold accents.

- **GO FOR ODD NUMBERS OVER EVEN** when choosing how many to pile on.

- **YOUR BRACELETS** shouldn't go past the middle of your forearm.

- **YOU CAN STACK ON BOTH WRISTS** at the same time, but if you do, don't match the two sides.

How to . . . Accessorize by Neckline

One of the biggest determining factors when it comes to what kind of accessories to wear is the neckline of your top or dress. Again, how you style yourself is subjective, and I've been proven wrong in the past. (I used to swear off necklaces with one-shoulder dresses until I saw Jennifer Lopez totally owning this look in Lanvin!) But here are some starter guidelines for what to wear with what cut:

- **CREW NECK.** Try a mid- to long-length necklace, or skip the necklace altogether and go with earrings instead. Shorter necklaces don't pop against this type of neckline, and the combination of the dual throat-hugging styles may give you a "choked" effect.

- **SCOOP NECK.** These look good paired with just about anything. Try different styles out to see what you like best!

- **V NECK.** If it's a deep V (and especially if you're larger-busted), skip the necklace and do an earring instead. With wider Vs that more closely resemble a portrait collar, you're free to add what you like.

- **BOAT NECK.** Avoid shorter necklaces, which will just get lost. Longer is better in this case.

- **BUTTON-DOWN.** I like the look of layered necklaces peeking out beneath an open collar (see opposite page for more) to give these masculine shirts a more feminine feel. Alternatively, you could button all the way up and top the look off with a bold necklace.

- **TURTLENECK.** No necklaces under any circumstance! Instead, opt for an earring or a bright lip as your sole accessory.

- **STRAPLESS.** Contrary to what you often see on red carpets or at formal functions, I don't personally like a short necklace with a strapless dress. I prefer to show off my décolletage with a great pair of earrings or a longer chain.

- **SWEETHEART.** There's enough visual interest in the shape of the neckline that a necklace would just distract the eye. Keep it simple and leave the chest bare. Earrings are acceptable if they're not overly complicated.

- **ONE SHOULDER.** As I said, I'm usually anti-necklace with this off-balance cut, but I've seen it done well with a short statement variety—just remember that your hair should be pulled back, away from your shoulders. When I wear this style of dress, I usually go for an earring instead.

How to . . . Layer Necklaces

Why wear one necklace when you could wear several? Fashion-forward women have been throwing monogamy out the window when it comes to their necklaces. I think this look can be really chic if done the right way, much like the arm-party trend, but don't overdo it or you'll risk looking like Mr. T. Here's what I recommend:

- **IF YOU'RE LAYERING PENDANTS, GIVE YOURSELF AN INCH AND A HALF BETWEEN TIERS.** If you clump them together or have them too far apart, the layering will look accidental.

- **DON'T BE AFRAID TO VARY THE METALS,** materials, and sizes for a richer effect.

- **THE CHUNKIER THE CHAIN,** the lower it should hang.

- **LAYER VARIOUS SHAPES**—a U shape with a V and a Y, for example.

- **FOR A CLASSIC, CAN'T-MISS LOOK,** use color as a unifying element.

GIVE YOUR CLOTHES
A MAKEOVER

Do you have an old piece of clothing that's just not cutting it anymore? Before you toss it or give it away, think creatively about how you could rework the garment into something that works for you. Sometimes a simple adjustment can give an old throwaway new life. Here are some ideas to get you started:

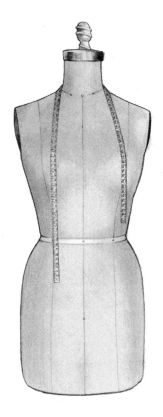

1. Change out the buttons on an old coat.
With just a couple of dollars and a few simple stitches, you've got a whole new look!

2. Stop drowning in your winter wear with some easy alterations.
Make a long winter coat flirtier by shortening it to peacoat length, or bring up the sleeves of a car-length coat so you can show off a pair of long leather gloves.

3. Make a mini out of a midi to show off your shapely legs!

4. Try shape-shifting by transforming an A-line skirt into a pencil cut.

5. Rather than letting an evening gown take up space in your closet, take *it* up instead—to a cocktail length, which will help you get more wear out of it.

6. Turn those old boyfriend jeans into cute cutoffs!
Just make sure they've got some give in the thigh.

7. Scratched the toes on your favorite pumps?
Use tape to section off the front and, using a Sharpie or spray paint, create a pair of DIY cap-toe shoes.

8. Take a baggy, shapeless dress and give it an elastic waist.
You can achieve the same look temporarily with a belt.

9. Got a cap-sleeve dress that makes you look like a linebacker?
Have the sleeves removed to reveal your shoulders for a sexier look.

10. Has a skirt become too short with age?
Find a fabric you like and add a panel along the bottom for a color-blocked effect.

OPPOSITES ATTRACT

I f there's anything that chocolate-covered pretzels have taught me, it's that sometimes two very different things that are great individually—like sweet and salty flavors—are actually better together. While it may not make sense in theory, in practice, unexpected pairings are a great way to carve out a style niche all your own. Not only does this "thinking outside the box" approach keep you from looking like a mannequin, but it helps you stretch out your wardrobe, too—allowing you the freedom to create countless combinations with your pieces.

I know this can be intimidating to put into practice, so to help push you, I'm giving you eight ideas for unlikely pairings that you can try on for size:

1. Vintage treasures + New finds
Example: a retro dress with a sexy stiletto heel
The secret to looking like you didn't just step off the set of *Mad Men* is to incorporate modern pieces with your thrifted goods.

2. Basics + Trends
Example: a white T-shirt with a statement necklace
Wearing every trend at once can be exhausting on the eyes. Give your attention-grabbing pieces a blank canvas by pairing them with something more traditional.

3. Sporty + Glam

Example: a sweatshirt with sequin embellishment
Avoid looking sloppy—or like you're trying too hard—by dressing up a sweatshirt (and dressing down your sparkle).

4. Preppy + Edgy

Example: a polo shirt with a leather skirt
What better way to give your everyday look a sexy edge than with a little leather?

5. High-end + Low-end

Example: Christian Louboutin shoes with Old Navy jeans
If you pick out your pieces right, no one should even be able to tell you shopped in the bargain bin. So why wouldn't you wear your expensive-looking jeans with actually expensive shoes?

6. Bohemian + Professional

Example: a flowy skirt with a tailored blazer
Avoid going full hippie chic by mixing in a structured jacket. This way you look ready for a night out on the town rather than a weekend at Woodstock.

7. Feminine + Masculine

Example: a tulle skirt with Chuck Taylors
A skirt fit for a fairy-tale princess worn with lace-up sneakers? You better believe it! This high-contrast look gets high marks for originality.

8. Neon + Pastels

Example: a neon green bandage skirt with a loose lavender tank

It's all about finding shades that work together, rather than having to stick to specific color families.

CHEAP CHICA CHALLENGE

Before I say good-bye, I want to turn the tables and give *you* a challenge. Below is a list of items many of you very well may have in your closet right now, and maybe you wear them often. But do you always wear them the exact same way, with the exact same things? I'm constantly amazed by how many women don't think to change up the way they wear a particular piece, simply because they're used to wearing it that way or because they bought it as part of an outfit. No more!

The best thing a Cheap Chica can do for her closet is to see all the possibilities a single garment has to offer. A pair of jeans can be dressed up enough to be worn to a fancy restaurant or dressed down enough to do yard work—it all depends on what you wear with them. So I'm going to challenge you to take the items in the following list and come up with three different ways to wear each piece. Include specific pieces you could pair it with and the variety of occasions you could wear your completed outfit to. This will get your brain thinking creatively so that you don't have to always buy a new outfit when an event arises—instead, you use what you've got to make the most of your wardrobe.

JEAN JACKET

Wear it with: _____ Wear it to: _____

_____ _____

_____ _____

_____ _____

SEQUIN SKIRT

Wear it with: _____ Wear it to: _____

_____ _____

_____ _____

_____ _____

PUFFY VEST

Wear it with: _____ Wear it to: _____

_____ _____

_____ _____

_____ _____

PRINTED PANTS

Wear it with: _____ Wear it to: _____

_____ _____

_____ _____

PEPLUM TOP

Wear it with: _____ Wear it to: _____

_____ _____

_____ _____

_____ _____

OK, OK, don't worry—I wasn't going to leave you completely on your own! I've styled these same items three totally different ways to help every one of you—from fashion novices to fashionistas—draw inspiration. To see my suggestions, turn to the photo insert.

• • •

W ell, Chicas, this is it—we've come to the end of our time together! I hope you've had as much fun learning my secrets for looking beautiful on a budget as I've enjoyed sharing them with you.

While I can't be with you in person, through this book, I'm with each of you in spirit, encouraging you to shop smart and dress like you give a damn! Now you can show the world how confident and capable you are with clothes that show off the best you—and that were purchased responsibly and styled flawlessly, of course. If you start to falter (and the best of us do) visit me at CheapChicas.com—where you'll find up-to-the-minute advice on trends, the latest red-carpet looks, and ideas to help you look like a million bucks for less—or refer to this book and review the lessons you've learned throughout these seven chapters:

1. Set a budget—and stick to it!

2. Take the time to find your own style and allow it to evolve.

3. An organized closet is the first step to a more functional wardrobe.

4. The best shoppers go in with a plan—and a list.

5. Know when to spend and when to save, and find the right balance for you.

6. Get the most for your money by using every dollar-saving resource available.

7. Style yourself like a pro by paying attention to the details.

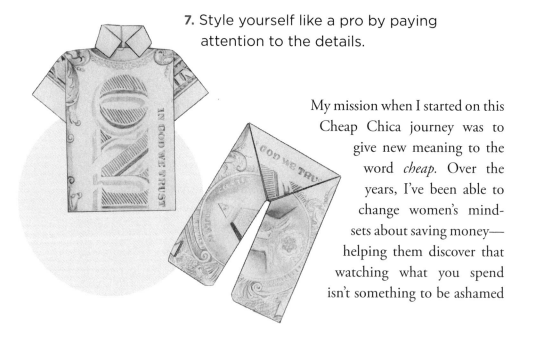

My mission when I started on this Cheap Chica journey was to give new meaning to the word *cheap*. Over the years, I've been able to change women's mindsets about saving money—helping them discover that watching what you spend isn't something to be ashamed of but rather celebrated. As you've read this book, I hope I've been able to do the same for you. I want you to be *proud* of your resourcefulness and always remember that money can't buy you style. With a little restraint, a little time, and a lot of creativity, anyone can look fabulous while still being frugal.

ACKNOWLEDGMENTS

What began as a simple way of sharing my love for fashion and "cheap treats" has become so much bigger than I could ever imagine—but it could not have happened without the support of these amazing people.

First, my incredible husband, Patrick. You have been so much more than just my partner in this journey. Thank you for being my sounding board, for keeping me sane, for drying my tears, and for always believing in me even when I didn't. This time in our life will forever remind me that two is always better than one, and I can't wait to discover and conquer our next challenge. Oh, and thank you for being such a passionate Eagles fan and attending the game on that fateful Sunday.

Mom, your unconditional love and strength have given me the courage and spirit to be who I am today. None of this is possible without you. Thank you for always being just a phone call away and for always making me feel so beautiful and special. You are my *tesoro*.

To my little brother, Edgar, thank you for making me a better sister and, in turn, a better person. I am so proud of you. To my Welita, your beauty and grace inspire me daily, and I'm so lucky to have inherited your sense of style! To Blanca, thank you for planting the seed and for nurturing me all those years. To my entire *familia, mil gracias*!

To Melissa, you are the sister I never had and my best friend. I will never forget all of the support, manual labor, and enthusiasm you have always shown for anything I have ever wanted to do, even those damn belts. And I promise, the next one is yours! To Sara, you are my oldest and dearest friend, and I can't imagine my world without your loyalty and friendship. Your energy is infectious, and I'm so lucky to have you in my life.

To Monica, I am so blessed to be part of your family and even luckier to call you a friend. Thank you for your wisdom, leadership, and advice. To Lauren, I can't get through the day without you. Thank you for your commitment to this book, to making everything perfect (just the way we like it), and yes, this is my way of asking you to stay forever.

To Jessica, thank you for making something so great out of simple words and ideas. You got me right from the beginning, and I know this is just the *beginning* for us. To Lina and Alison, thank you for contributing so much beauty and creativity to the pages of this book. To my editor, Marisa, you have made this process so easy and enjoyable. Thank you for making me feel like a writer and like I could actually do this. To one of my favorite Texans and literary agent, David, thank you for pulling my story from the pages of a newspaper and for seeing the potential in this project. You have been my beacon on this road, and I only wish I could have ten more of you on my team. To Ashley and Stephanie, thank you for believing in me and for always having my back.

Lastly, to each and every one of my readers, words cannot express my gratitude. Y'all are my constant source of inspiration and the reason any of this is even possible. Thank you for helping turn this Texas girl's dreams into reality.

ABOUT THE
AUTHOR

Lilliana Vazquez, founder and creative director of CheapChicas.com, is one of the most sought-after style experts in the fashion industry. Lilliana makes regular appearances on the *Today* show, *The Rachael Ray Show*, and *E! News*, where she shares her frugally fashionable point of view with audiences nationally. She has been featured in publications like *People Style Watch*, *Lucky*, and *Elle*. Lilliana is also a host on *New York Live* on NBC New York, where she covers fashion and entertainment and is a fixture on the red carpet. She lives in Philadelphia with her husband and is originally from Fort Worth, Texas.